A GOOD RECIPE BEHAVES.

It makes you a promise and keeps it.

And when you cook a good recipe, you learn from it—and add it to your repertoire. It's like a musician learning a new favorite tune: a favorite recipe becomes a part of you.

I've cooked my entire life to develop this repertoire, and I'm giving it to you: rock-solid, never-fail recipes that are more rewarding than demanding. These are recipes you can trust and use and reuse, recipes with a wide range of flavors and lots of ways to shake them up.

The food here is what I'd serve if you walked in the door tonight. It isn't fancy, but it is special.

So go ahead, riff a little. Turn my repertoire into your own.

Jessica

Repertoire

Repertoire

ALL THE RECIPES YOU NEED

Jessica Battilana
Photographs by Ed Anderson

LITTLE, BROWN AND COMPANY

New York | Boston | London

Little, Brown and Company
Hachette Book Group
1290 Avenue of the Americas, New York, NY 10104
littlebrown.com

First Edition: April 2018

Little, Brown and Company is a division of Hachette Book Group, Inc.
The Little, Brown name and logo are trademarks of Hachette Book Group, Inc.

The publisher is not responsible for websites (or their content) that are not owned by the publisher.

The Hachette Speakers Bureau provides a wide range of authors for speaking events. To find out more, go to hachettespeakersbureau.com or call (866) 376-6591.

Lyrics from "Raised on Robbery": words and music by Joni Mitchell. Copyright © 1973 (Renewed) Crazy Crow Music. All Rights Administered by Sony/ATV Music Publishing, 8 Music Square West, Nashville, TN 37203. All Rights Reserved. Used by permission of Alfred Music.

All photographs by Ed Anderson, except those on pages 4, 238, and 240, which are by Molly DeCoudreaux.
Design by Toni Tajima

ISBN 978-0-316-36034-0
LCCN 2017954592

10 9 8 7 6 5 4 3 2 1

LSC-C

Printed in the United States of America

Hey, Mama.
This one's for you.

Remember.

Contents

Ways to Start

Mains

Sweets

I'm a pretty good cook
I'm sitting on my groceries
Come up to my kitchen
I'll show you my best recipe.

JONI MITCHELL, "RAISED ON ROBBERY"

Repertoire

Building a Repertoire

There's a three-hour stretch between picking up our two young boys from school and settling them into their beds for the night that my wife and I call running the gauntlet.

We're all tired, Sarah and me and the kids, who, having shed shoes and clothing in a trail from the front door to the kitchen, are agitating for attention and dinner. In the old days, before the kids, I might have leisurely pulled a cookbook from the shelf, browsed through for inspiration, and hit the store for ingredients. I'd try a new recipe, tweaking it until it was just right; Sarah and I would eat long after dark. But it's different now. Kids, work, life…I just don't have the time I used to spend dreaming up dinner. No one does.

So what's the solution? Friends who'd had children before me promised a future of takeout and cereal for dinner. But I'm stubborn. Instead of giving up on cooking at home, I doubled down on it. I discovered that the trick—if you can call it that—was to develop and cook from my own repertoire, my set of durable, flexible recipes that now form the backbone of my cooking life.

Musicians have their own repertoires— the pieces they'll always know how to play, from wedding marches to funeral dirges, without looking at sheet music. It's the same for a cook. Repertoire recipes are what I serve for both weeknight suppers and dinner parties, the meals that I feed to my sons, the familiar favorites I reach for when it's time to celebrate.

They are real recipes from real life, and they really work.

The truth is that home cooks don't need hundreds of recipes in their arsenals. A few dozen good ones and the knowledge and freedom that cooking them frequently gives you are all you really need.

A good recipe behaves; it makes you a promise and keeps it. It turns you into a magician capable of transforming ingredients into a meal that has you doing one of those little kitchen dances between stove and sink. A good recipe never grows old—it changes with you.

I've cooked my entire life to develop this repertoire, and it's damn good. I'm giving them to you, these rock-solid, never-fail recipes, ones that are more rewarding than demanding. These are recipes you can trust and use and reuse, recipes with a wide range of flavors and lots of ways to shake them up. They range from curried noodles to a maple-blueberry cornmeal cake to flank steak with salsa verde and bucatini all'Amatriciana. They may not appear to have much in common, but a repertoire should be diverse, because that's how all of us want to cook and eat, choosing our dinner based on what sounds good to us and what we've got time to make. It should have keepers you can cook for the rest of your life.

The recipes in this book are meant to last, which means they also invite adaptation. The more you cook these recipes, the more they become yours. You'll get better at making them, and faster, too, and the recipes will transform into something highly personal. They taste great, but they will also give you something more than a simple meal.

When nothing else is turning out the way you'd hoped, it can be reassuring to know that your pot of tortilla soup will. I've experienced this myself. When my first son was born and then again when our second arrived, when everything felt upside down and I was sleeping in forty-five-minute increments, the kitchen was a refuge. I may not have known how to calm an inconsolable baby at four a.m., but I knew that with a couple of cans of tomatoes, some olive oil, garlic, and time, I could make a marinara to toss on spaghetti that my wife and I could eat from the pot, happy, baby on the hip.

That marinara is in this book. The food here is what we really eat at home, what I'd serve you if you walk in the door tonight. It isn't fancy, but it *is* special.

I organized it as simply as I could, the way we actually think about what to eat: starters for a meal or a party, then main courses, and finally desserts. You could take a recipe from each chapter and string them together into a three-course meal, or you might find that a wedge of Cheater's Tortilla Española (page 61) and a salad are all you want. Or, after a bad day, maybe a Negroni and a bowl of Potato Chips (page 77) on the couch will do the trick. Can you eat Apricot-Nectarine Crisp (page 174) for breakfast? Oh yeah. Does leftover Lamb Ragù with Creamy Polenta (page 124) or a reheated Broccoli Rabe and Mozzarella Calzone (page 121) make a killer lunch the next day? Yes, and yes.

I'm a recipe writer, but I'm not much for rules. I've designed this book to be flexible, and within each recipe, I've tried to answer the questions I know my friends would ask if they were making something for the first time, things like *Can you substitute this for that? Can you make it ahead? Can you freeze it? What should I serve it with?* After cooking a recipe as written, you'll probably have your own ideas too.

Go ahead, riff a little. Turn my repertoire into your own.

Cooking by Heart
(Or, A Little About Me)

When I was a kid, I would often imagine that I'd been asked to participate in a talent show. As I considered my hypothetical performance, I'd review my "talents": I was wildly uncoordinated, a terrible dancer, and had a mediocre voice.

But I could cook. In the talent show of my dreams, I took the stage and, modeling my act after videos of Julia Child stooping next to Jacques Pépin, demonstrated how to make perfect scrambled eggs. I'd practice, using the window behind the stove in our kitchen as my mirror. After dark I'd watch my reflection as I stirred and sautéed, explaining every step as I went.

My mother was a devoted home cook. After her children were grown, she took a course at the Culinary Institute of America in Napa and returned to Vermont ready for a second act. She started working in the kitchen at a specialty food market in my hometown; twenty years later, she retired as its co-owner. But before she became a professional, she cooked every night, pulling from a repertoire so deep, I don't recall her ever cracking a cookbook.

Birthdays meant cake; holidays meant standing rib roasts and bacon-draped turkeys. We'd look forward to the late-summer day when we'd buy ears of freshly picked corn to boil and butter. When we finished stacking wood for the winter, we'd celebrate with popcorn balls and hot apple cider. In spring, after we braved the muddy back roads of Vermont in an old station wagon, we'd earn a trip to the sugar shack to sip from enamel mugs of golden maple syrup. Food provided the rhythm and ritual by which we lived our lives.

I went to college and got a history degree. But like Mom, I couldn't stop cooking.

I worked as a cashier at a renowned specialty grocer in Cambridge. Then I earned a summer internship at La Varenne, a cooking school in the French countryside run by Anne Willan, a contemporary of Julia Child. There I cooked daily, testing recipes, making giant meals for visitors, and, under Willan's exacting tutelage, learning how to make French classics, from *babas au rhum* to delicate fish mousse.

Back home, I worked as a private chef, writing a bit on the side, before moving to California. There I found a job at Chez Panisse, not as a cook but as a reservationist. Lunch was the perk I stuck around for: giant green salads, the tender lettuces the stuff of food-writer dreams; squares of chocolate pavé, a flourless cake with a crackling top; slices of leftover lamb anointed in grass-green aioli or salsa verde that I adored so much, I added them to my burgeoning repertoire.

Those staff meals—and watching the chefs prepare the food for service each night—influenced how I cooked at home. Inspired by what I saw at the restaurant, I'd shop at the farmers' market, and suddenly I was part of a community of young people who put food front and center, like my family always had.

I still had the ambition to write, though, and left Chez Panisse for a job at *Sunset* magazine's test kitchen. From *Sunset,* I took a job at a San Francisco–based city magazine, working the food and restaurant beat. For four years I immersed myself in restaurant culture, dining at every new restaurant, meeting nearly every chef in town. Another similar job followed, and I continued to write stories about restaurants and chefs.

When the opportunity arose to work with Charles Phan, chef-owner of the Slanted Door, on his first cookbook, *Vietnamese Home Cooking,* I jumped at the chance. More cookbook collaborations followed, and my role was always clear: it was my job to be the voice of the home cook, reminding the professionals that the average person has neither a grain mill nor a chinois nor a reliable source of vadouvan or black garlic. And along the way I picked up tips, tricks, ideas, and recipes that further refined my own repertoire.

And that's how I got to this point, ready to hand over my best recipes. They're the ones I trust, the ones I cook by heart. After nearly two decades of cooking and writing about food, I realize that I'm finally in a place to share what I've learned. I'm still in the kitchen after all these years, still hungry.

A Word About Ingredients

Unless I say otherwise, in my house and in these recipes, these are the ingredients I use:

The **milk** is whole (or at least not skim). The **butter** is unsalted. The **yogurt** and **sour cream** are full fat. The **salt** is Diamond Crystal kosher unless I'm using flaky sea salt for a little crunch on top, and then it's Maldon. The **mayonnaise** is Hellmann's, or Best Foods, as it's called out west. (You can fight me on this, but I am right!)

For everyday **olive oil**, I get Tiger brand, an inexpensive Tuscan oil that comes in a three-liter tin, or the good stuff from California Olive Ranch, milled near my home. For salads, I keep a fruity olive oil on hand; taste a few different brands and find your favorite. Once a year, I buy a bottle of olio nuovo; this fiery, freshly pressed green oil is spicy! I drizzle it on chopped raw fennel, on beans, and into soup. And I usually have a **nut oil**, like walnut, around for salad dressings.

Treat yourself to a big chunk of **Parmigiano-Reggiano** if you're able. Having it in my cheese drawer is like a security blanket. You can find good-quality Parm in big blocks at Costco; two pounds might seem like a lot, but it keeps well and goes fast.

For **feta**, use the kind made with sheep's milk if you can find it. Sheep's milk has more fat than cow's or goat's milk, so the feta made from it is richer and creamier. If you can get it packed in brine, great. Avoid buying those cartons of pre-crumbled feta (or blue cheese). Not only are they more expensive, but the cheese is often drier. Besides, crumbling cheese is not exactly an advanced skill—you can do this.

My favorite **dried pasta** is Rustichella d'Abruzzo, an Italian brand that is extruded through bronze dies, which gives the pasta a rough texture that helps sauce cling to it. It's more expensive than most grocery-store brands (and might require a trip to a specialty market), but it's worth it.

In my kitchen I have both **oil-** and **salt-packed anchovies**. The oil-packed anchovies are already filleted, so they're easy to use straight from the tin. Salt-packed anchovies are the whole fish (minus the heads) packed into coarse salt. Before you use them you have to soak them in water for about thirty minutes, then fillet them with your fingers. Why go through the hassle? Generally, salt-packed anchovies are meatier than the oil-packed fillets, with a more pronounced flavor. I like them both, and they can be used interchangeably in all the recipes in the book. **Anchovy paste** in a tube is also a great invention, and there's no waste. A quarter teaspoon of the paste is equal to about one anchovy fillet.

Capers are available packed in either brine or salt. The benefit of the brined ones is that they're ready to use—just drain and toss them in. The salted capers must be soaked in water to cover for about thirty minutes. I often opt for the convenience of brined, but that convenience comes at a small cost, which is that the vinegar in the brine changes the flavor of the capers somewhat; salted capers, by contrast, have a less piquant (though still very big) flavor. Again, they can be used interchangeably in these recipes.

I use **chocolate** and **cocoa** from Guittard, which is produced near my San Francisco home by some really nice folks who let me watch chocolate chips being made. Valrhona chocolate and cocoa are also great.

I have never been a churchgoer, but every Sunday I do go to the **farmers' market**, where I get the majority of the **fruits, vegetables,** and **nuts** we eat. It makes me feel good—you might even say spiritually enriched—to buy food directly from the people who make it, and it turns something that could be a chore (food shopping) into a social outing. I've gotten my kids into it now, too, luring them with the promise of samples and pastries.

I pay attention to how my **meat** and **fish** are raised and I have come to terms with paying more for the good stuff. That means we eat less of it or that I use lesser cuts, ground meat, or whole chickens, bones and all. We also eat a lot of **beans**.

I usually try to plan about three meals at a time. A week's worth feels like too many (both to plan for and shop for), and I can't always predict at the start of the week what I'll feel like eating at the end. Often, I'll make a big batch of something (meatballs, beans, chile-braised beef, tart dough, salad dressing) and save or freeze a portion of it for a second meal. I'm not talking long storage—I'm frequently ready to revisit it (gratefully) the following week. It helps to always keep **basics**— **potatoes, onions, carrots, dried** or **canned beans, eggs** and **cheese, canned tomatoes**—on hand. You'll see that a lot of the recipes in this book call for ingredients you probably already have in the kitchen. And if they're not in your kitchen, they're readily available at a regular grocery store.

Ways to Start

The Greenest Green Salad

Serves 4 to 6

2 oil-packed anchovy fillets

½ cup mayonnaise, preferably Hellmann's/Best Foods

⅓ cup full-fat Greek yogurt

½ cup parsley leaves

¼ cup basil leaves

1 tablespoon lemon juice, plus additional for seasoning

2 tablespoons finely chopped fresh tarragon leaves

2 tablespoons minced chives

Kosher salt and freshly ground black pepper

2 cups snap peas

2 hearts of romaine lettuce, washed and chopped into bite-size pieces

2 Persian or Japanese cucumbers, diced

3 green onions, thinly sliced

1 avocado, cubed

I AM NOT SURE that I want to live in a world where ranch dressing is more beloved than Green Goddess, which is superior in both name and taste, so I'm doing everything in my power to bring this vibrant, herb-packed green dressing into the limelight.

Green Goddess is a kitchen MVP. It can be used as a salad dressing, yes, but it's also a dip for crudités, a marinade for grilled chicken, and, if you're one of the weirdos who like to do this, it's great on pizza or with French fries too.

For this super-green salad, I combine crunchy romaine, cucumbers, snap peas, green onions, and avocado, then douse it with the irresistible dressing.

―――

> In a food processor combine the anchovy fillets, mayonnaise, yogurt, parsley, basil, and 1 tablespoon lemon juice and process until smooth and brilliant green. Transfer to a lidded jar, stir in the tarragon and chives, and season to taste with salt, pepper, and additional lemon juice.

> Bring a medium saucepan of salted water to a boil over high heat. Add the snap peas and cook until just tender, about 2 minutes. Drain in a colander and rinse with cold water until the peas are completely cool. Transfer to a paper-towel-lined plate to dry (the dressing won't stick to a wet snap pea). Cut each pea in half crosswise on the bias.

> In a large bowl, combine the snap peas, romaine, cucumbers, and green onions and mix well to combine. Add the avocado and about half the dressing (save the rest for another salad; it will keep, covered and refrigerated, for up to a week). Mix gently with your hands until the salad is well coated with dressing, adding more if necessary. Season with salt and freshly ground black pepper and serve cold.

Sam's Spring Fattoush Salad

Serves 4 to 6

2 pieces lavash bread

¼ cup plus 3 tablespoons extra-virgin olive oil

Kosher salt

Aleppo pepper (optional)

¼ cup lemon juice

1 clove garlic, peeled and minced

5 Persian, Armenian, or Japanese cucumbers, thinly sliced

5 radishes, thinly sliced

3 green onions, thinly sliced

1 cup dill fronds

1 cup mint leaves

½ cup feta, preferably sheep's milk

A FEW WEEKS after our older son was born, I ran into my friend Sam Mogannam. I was light-headed from exhaustion, teary from lack of sleep. "You want some advice about kids?" asked Sam, who has two daughters. I figured he was going to tell me what I'd already heard—to sleep when the baby was sleeping or purchase a specific brand of pacifier. Instead he grabbed my hand, looked straight into my eyes, and said, simply, "Surrender."

It remains the best parenting advice I've heard, and it's the only tip I share with new parents.

In addition to being a font of wisdom, Sam's a great cook; he's co-owner of Bi-Rite Market, a beloved San Francisco grocery store started by his grandfather, and before taking over the family business, he worked in restaurants. This is an approximation of a simple recipe he served me once. Though it's simple, the devil is in the details. Thin-skinned Persian, Armenian, or Japanese cucumbers, which have few seeds, a snappy texture, and a distinct sweetness, are what make the salad special. In a pinch, European hothouse cucumbers can be substituted, but avoid the typical grocery-store cukes, which are too seedy and wet for this recipe.

Part of what makes this salad so great is the dynamic textures; the cracker-like baked lavash croutons and the crunchy cucumbers and radishes contrast with the creamy feta and soft herbs. I dress this with an especially tart vinaigrette made from equal parts lemon juice and olive oil and serve it right away, before it gets soggy. It would be a great side dish with all sorts of things, but I particularly like it alongside the Grilled Tahini Chicken on page 93.

> Preheat the oven to 350°F. Brush the lavash on both sides with 3 tablespoons of the olive oil. Arrange on a baking sheet and sprinkle with salt and Aleppo pepper, if using. Transfer to the oven and bake until golden and crisp, 8 to 10 minutes. Remove from the oven and let cool.

> In a small bowl, whisk together the lemon juice, garlic, and a generous pinch of salt. Whisk in the remaining ¼ cup olive oil until combined.

> In a large salad bowl, combine the cucumbers, radishes, green onions, dill, and mint. Drizzle half of the dressing over it and toss with your hands to coat. Break the lavash into bite-size pieces and add to the bowl along with the feta. Drizzle over the remaining dressing and gently mix with your hands to combine. Season to taste with additional salt and Aleppo pepper and serve immediately.

Gribiche
with
Asparagus

Serves 4 to 6

2 bunches medium asparagus
(about 2 pounds)

2 large eggs

1 clove garlic, peeled

2 teaspoons Dijon mustard

2 tablespoons white wine
vinegar or lemon juice

8 cornichon pickles

1 tablespoon capers

½ cup mild extra-virgin
olive oil

2 tablespoons finely
chopped flat-leaf parsley

2 tablespoons finely
chopped chives

¾ teaspoon kosher salt

¼ teaspoon freshly ground
black pepper

THERE IS NO ONE perfect recipe for gribiche sauce, and I happen to find almost all variations on it—from the thick, mayonnaise-y versions to ones that are more like chunky vinaigrettes—absolutely irresistible. The combination of eggs and mustard recalls the flavor of deviled eggs, which I love, and the hit of acidity (from the vinegar, cornichons, and capers) and the abundance of green herbs make it taste bright and fresh. To allow those ingredients to shine, use a mild olive oil that won't overshadow them.

The sauce is especially good with asparagus. I like the medium spears; the pencil-thin ones are too floppy, the thick ones too fibrous. It's also good on boiled potatoes, poached chicken, poached salmon, even cold cuts. Serve this as a first course or a side dish.

> Trim the woody base off each asparagus spear, and, if you're feeling fancy, peel the bottom third of each spear with a vegetable peeler (it makes the spears look nicer but doesn't really affect the taste). Bring a large pot of salted water to a boil over high heat, and while the water heats, prepare an ice bath and set it nearby. Add the asparagus to the boiling water and cook until just tender, 3 to 4 minutes. Using tongs, transfer the asparagus to the ice bath. Once they're cool, transfer to a baking sheet lined with paper towels or a clean kitchen towel. Do not dump the ice bath.

> Return the water to a boil and carefully lower in the eggs. Boil the eggs for 7 minutes, then use a slotted spoon to transfer them to the ice bath (adding additional ice if necessary). When they are cool enough to handle, peel them. Put the peeled eggs in the bowl of a food processor and add the garlic, mustard, white wine vinegar, cornichons, and capers. Pulse until the eggs are coarsely chopped. With the food processor running, drizzle in the olive oil and continue processing until the sauce is creamy. Transfer to a bowl and stir in the parsley, chives, salt, and pepper.

> To serve, spoon the sauce onto a large platter and arrange the asparagus on top, or serve the gribiche sauce in a bowl alongside a pile of the asparagus and dip the spears into it.

Mr. Ellis's Tomato Tart

Makes one 10-inch tart

FOR THE CRUST:

2½ cups all-purpose flour

1½ teaspoons kosher salt

1 cup cold unsalted butter, cut into ½-inch cubes

¼ cup ice water

FOR THE FILLING:

1 cup mayonnaise, preferably Hellmann's/Best Foods

½ cup buttermilk

2 large eggs

¾ cup grated Parmigiano-Reggiano

6 green onions, white and light green parts only, finely chopped

¼ teaspoon freshly ground black pepper

3 medium tomatoes, cored and cut into ¼-inch wedges, or 2 medium tomatoes, cored and cut into ¼-inch wedges, plus ½ cup cherry tomatoes, halved

½ cup fresh basil leaves

THIS SAVORY TART is not named for my son Ellis but for a chef I met a few years back, Cole Ellis (my son isn't named for him either). At that time he was cooking at Capitol Grille in Nashville; he now owns the Delta Meat Market in his hometown of Cleveland, Mississippi.

Mr. Ellis, a soft-spoken Southerner, took me on a tour of Nashville in his pickup truck, promised me a biscuit-making lesson (I'm still waiting), and created this recipe for a tart with a buttery crust, a righteous mayonnaise-buttermilk-Parmigiano custard, and loads of tomatoes. Though it probably goes without saying, this stunner should be made only in deep summer, when you can get the best, juiciest tomatoes in all different colors and sizes. I like to use a mixture of larger tomatoes cut into wedges or thick slices and halved cherry tomatoes. Serve this tart as a first course or for lunch or dinner with some dressed arugula alongside.

> Combine the flour and salt in the bowl of a food processor and pulse to combine. Add the butter cubes and pulse until the pieces of butter are the size of small peas. Pour in the ice water and pulse until the dough comes together in a shaggy ball. Turn the dough out onto a sheet of plastic wrap, use the plastic wrap to gather the dough into a ball, then flatten it into a disk with the heel of your hand. Tightly wrap and chill for at least 1 hour and up to 3 days. (The dough can be frozen for up to a month. Let thaw overnight in the refrigerator before using.)

> Preheat the oven to 350°F. Place the chilled dough on a lightly floured cutting board and lightly flour your rolling pin. Roll the dough into a 14-inch circle about ¼ inch thick. Transfer the dough to a high-sided 10-inch removable-bottom tart pan, fitting the dough into the bottom and along the sides of the pan. (If you don't own a deep tart pan with a removable bottom, the pie can be baked in a deep-dish glass or ceramic pie plate instead.) Use your rolling pin to roll over the top edges of the pan, trimming the overhanging dough. Refrigerate for 10 minutes.

RECIPE CONTINUES ↘

> Remove the tart pan from the refrigerator. Use a fork to prick the bottom of the dough all over, then place a 14-inch sheet of parchment paper or aluminum foil into the tart pan. Add enough dried beans or pie weights to weigh the paper down, place the tart pan on a rimmed baking sheet (this makes it easier to retrieve from the oven without damaging the crust), and bake until the edges of the crust are firm and beginning to turn golden, about 15 minutes. Remove the pan from the oven and carefully remove the pie weights and parchment paper or aluminum foil. Return the pan to the oven and continue to bake until the crust is golden, about 10 to 15 minutes longer.

> In a large bowl, whisk together the mayonnaise, buttermilk, eggs, 1/2 cup of the grated Parmigiano, the green onions, and the black pepper. Pour three-quarters of the mixture into the parbaked crust, then arrange the tomato wedges (and cherry tomatoes, if using) in a circular pattern on top of the mixture, overlapping them slightly. Roughly tear the basil leaves with your fingers and distribute the basil evenly over the top of the tart. Pour the remaining custard over and sprinkle with the remaining 1/4 cup Parmigiano.

> Bake the tart until the crust is a deep golden brown and the filling is set and beginning to brown on top, about 30 minutes. Transfer to a cooling rack and let cool at least 30 minutes, then unmold the tart and cut into wedges. Serve warm or at room temperature.

Bean Salad *with* Cherry Tomatoes *and* Aioli

MANY YEARS AGO, my friend Chris Kronner was cooking at Bar Tartine, a restaurant in San Francisco (now closed). During the era when he was the chef, I spent a lot of time sitting at the long marble bar because Chris—tall, with a head of wild curls and a wry sense of humor—was always making something I wanted to eat. I almost always prefer cooking at home to eating out, but the restaurants I love best work hard to make you feel like you're part of the family. That's how it was at Bar Tartine in those days when I'd swing by for a glass of wine and an omelet or a spectacular burger (Chris went on to open his own burger-centric restaurant, KronnerBurger, in Oakland). But the dish I couldn't get enough of was a bean salad that Chris would make toward the end of the summer when shelling beans, green beans, and tomatoes were all abundant at the market.

Shelling beans are beans that are normally grown for drying but can also be cooked fresh. They're sold in their pods and must be shelled before cooking, though because they're fresh, the cooking time is much shorter than for dried beans. Because of their relatively brief season, a farmers' market is likely the best place to find them.

Chris fussed over that salad. It always had a few varieties of shelling beans, cooked separately and perfectly, and the crowning glory was a spoonful of aioli, which blended with the vinaigrette that was dressing the beans to form the most luscious sauce.

At the shower for our first baby, my wife and I asked each of our friends to write a note to our future child—a piece of advice, maybe, something he could read when he was older and wondering about his parents' life before he arrived. After the party, I pulled out Chris's card. On it, he'd written the recipe for the shelling bean salad. At the end of the final step, he wrote, *Add a large spoonful of aioli and watch Mom's face light up.*

To simplify the recipe a bit, I use just one type of shelling bean, partly because one is usually all I can find, even at the farmers' market, and partly because if you use an assortment, you really should cook them separately, which is sort of tedious (and you've already committed to shelling beans, so let's not push it). If you can't find shelling beans, just use an assortment of string beans, like green, wax, and Romano. You could also use drained, rinsed canned beans, like cannellini—

they're not a substitute for fresh shelling beans, exactly, but they'll work in a pinch.

You can make all the components of this salad ahead of time, but don't combine the beans and vinaigrette until just before you plan to serve it or the green beans will discolor.

————

> Put the shelling beans in a large heavy saucepan or Dutch oven and add water to cover by 2 inches. Add the bay leaf, garlic, a glug of olive oil, and a few teaspoons of salt. Bring to a boil over medium-high heat, then reduce heat and simmer until the beans are tender, about 30 minutes. Remove five beans from the liquid and taste them; if any of the beans are underdone, continue cooking until all five beans in your next sample are tender. Drain and discard the bay leaf and garlic.

> Bring a medium saucepan of salted water to a boil over high heat. Add the haricots verts and cook until just tender, about 4 minutes. Drain in a colander and rinse with cold water until the beans are completely cool. Transfer to a paper-towel-lined plate to dry (the dressing won't stick to a wet bean).

> In a small bowl, whisk together the mustard and a pinch of salt. Whisk in the vinegar, then whisk in the ¼ cup olive oil until combined.

> In a large bowl, combine the drained shelling beans, blanched haricots verts, and cherry tomatoes. Add the oregano and thyme, pour the vinaigrette over, and toss to coat. Season to taste with additional salt. Transfer to bowls and top each serving with a generous spoonful of aioli. Serve immediately.

Serves 4 to 6

3 cups shelled fresh shelling beans, such as cranberry or cannellini (about 3 pounds in the pod)

1 bay leaf

1 clove garlic, peeled and crushed

¼ cup extra-virgin olive oil, plus additional for boiling the beans

Kosher salt

12 ounces haricots verts, small green beans, or a mixture of green and wax beans

1 teaspoon Dijon mustard

2 tablespoons sherry or red wine vinegar

2 cups cherry tomatoes, halved

2 teaspoons chopped fresh oregano

1 teaspoon chopped fresh thyme leaves

½ cup Aioli (page 35) or Fancy Mayonnaise (page 62), for serving

EVEN AFTER YEARS of making aioli, I'm still impressed with myself when I produce a batch. The process still feels like magic. For all the bluster about how difficult it can be, all the warnings about "broken" emulsions, making garlic mayonnaise from scratch is actually quite simple and incredibly satisfying.

The key is to add the oil very, very slowly at the start. When I say "drop by drop," that's really what I mean. If you swamp the yolk with too much oil at the outset, you'll never get a nice emulsion and your aioli will never thicken. Use a measuring cup to help control the flow of oil; I tip mine just enough that droplets collect on the pouring spout, then drip in. The process is sort of like rubbing your tummy while you pat your head, so it can be helpful to make it a two-person gig until you get the hang of it; one person whisks while the other controls the flow of oil. A dollop of aioli improves many things—fried potatoes, steamed vegetables, and canned tuna, for a start. Make some and you'll find ways to use it.

Aioli

Makes about 1 cup

1 egg yolk

1 cup mild-flavored olive oil (or a 50-50 mix of grapeseed or canola oil and olive oil)

1 clove garlic, peeled

Kosher salt

Lemon juice

> Set a medium mixing bowl on a kitchen towel (this will prevent the bowl from spinning as you whisk). Put the yolk in the bowl and whisk well. Pour the olive oil into a measuring cup and, whisking constantly, begin adding the oil to the yolk, drop by drop at first, until the mixture begins to thicken and emulsify.

> Continue adding the olive oil in a thin, steady stream, whisking constantly, until all the oil has been added and the mixture is thick but spreadable. If the aioli becomes too thick or looks greasy, add a tablespoon or two of warm water to smooth and thin it. If the mixture hasn't thickened, this means your mayonnaise has broken. Don't panic! Put another egg yolk in a clean, dry bowl. Pour your broken mayonnaise into a measuring cup and, whisking constantly, add the broken mayonnaise to the egg yolk drop by drop (having screwed it up the first time, you'll probably take extra care not to add it too quickly the second go-round!).

> Pound the garlic and a pinch of salt into a paste using a mortar and pestle (if you don't have a mortar and pestle, use the side of your knife to crush the garlic into a paste). Stir the pounded garlic into the aioli and season to taste with additional salt and lemon juice. The aioli will keep, covered and refrigerated, for several days.

FANCY TOASTS

W<small>E ARE LIVING IN</small> the peak toast era, if you believe the food magazines, but the truth is that toast has always been one of my favorite foods. When I was a kid, I liked lightly toasted Pepperidge Farm white bread buttered edge to edge and showered with cinnamon sugar. I still like that, but I have also developed an appreciation for salty, oil-slicked pieces of toasted baguette onto which I pile all sorts of delicious things, from canned sardines to mashed hard-boiled eggs and sliced avocado.

Really, you can put anything you want on top of toast, but these are my favorite vegetarian combinations. If you make all three, you'll have an especially beautiful assortment.

Makes about 20 toasts

FOR THE TOASTS:

1 baguette, cut diagonally into ⅓-inch-thick slices

Extra-virgin olive oil, for brushing

Kosher salt and freshly ground black pepper

1 clove garlic, peeled

——

> Preheat the oven to 350°F. Arrange the slices of baguette on a rimmed baking sheet in a single layer. With a pastry brush, brush each toast on both sides with olive oil and season with salt and pepper. Transfer to the oven and bake until crisp but not brown, about 10 minutes. Remove from the oven. Rub the garlic over the surface of each toast once. Let cool. Toasts are best the same day they're made.

Garlicky Broccoli Rabe *and* Provolone

1 bunch broccoli rabe, ends trimmed

2 tablespoons extra-virgin olive oil, plus more for drizzling

2 cloves garlic, peeled and slivered

¼ teaspoon red pepper flakes

Kosher salt

20 toasts (at left)

2 ounces aged provolone or Pecorino Romano cheese

——

> Bring a large pot of salted water to a boil. Add the broccoli rabe and boil until just tender, about 5 minutes. Drain. When cool enough to handle, squeeze the broccoli rabe hard over the sink to remove any excess liquid and transfer to a cutting board. Finely chop the broccoli rabe. Pour the 2 tablespoons of olive oil into a medium frying pan over medium heat. Add the garlic and red pepper flakes and cook, stirring, until the garlic is aromatic, about 30 seconds (do not let it brown). Add the chopped broccoli rabe and stir to coat with the olive oil; cook 3 minutes, until silky. Season to taste with salt. Spoon some of the mixture onto each piece of toast and use a vegetable peeler to shave some cheese over the top of each. Drizzle with additional olive oil.

Roasted Tomatoes *and* Ricotta

1 pound small tomatoes, such as Early Girls, cored and halved, or cherry tomatoes, halved

¼ cup extra-virgin olive oil

2 cloves garlic, peeled and slivered

Kosher salt and freshly ground black pepper

2 sprigs fresh thyme

1 cup whole-milk ricotta

½ teaspoon lemon zest

20 toasts (facing page)

———

> Preheat the oven to 375°F. Put the tomatoes in a baking dish, cut-side down, and drizzle with the olive oil. Sprinkle the garlic over, tucking it between the tomatoes, and season with salt and pepper. Add the thyme sprigs. Transfer to the oven and bake until the tomatoes are soft and slumped, about 30 minutes (if you're using cherry tomatoes, begin checking them after 15 minutes; they won't take as long as the larger Early Girls). Remove from the oven and let cool. The tomatoes can be made ahead; they can sit at room temperature for a few hours or refrigerated, covered, for up to a day. Let them return to room temperature before using.

> In a small bowl stir together the ricotta and lemon zest. Season to taste with salt and pepper. Spoon some of the ricotta on the crostini, then spoon some of the roasted tomato juices from the baking dish onto the ricotta and top each with a tomato half.

Pea Smash *and* Marinated Feta

½ cup feta, preferably sheep's milk

½ cup extra-virgin olive oil

1 teaspoon fresh thyme leaves

¼ teaspoon red pepper flakes

Zest and juice of 1 lemon

1 cup shelled fresh or frozen peas

5 mint leaves

1 teaspoon kosher salt

20 toasts (facing page)

Freshly ground black pepper

———

> Crumble the feta into large pieces over a bowl and add ¼ cup of the olive oil, the thyme, red pepper flakes, and lemon zest. Stir gently to combine and let stand 30 minutes. (The marinated feta can be made ahead; wrap tightly and refrigerate for up to 3 days and let come to room temperature before using.)

> Bring a small saucepan of salted water to a boil. Add the peas and cook until just tender, about 5 minutes. Drain and transfer to the bowl of a food processor. Add the remaining ¼ cup olive oil, mint, salt, and lemon juice and pulse into a chunky mash.

> Spread some of the pea mash on the crostini and top each with some of the marinated feta and freshly ground black pepper.

Sweet Corn Fritters

Makes 15 fritters

FOR THE FRITTERS:

1 cup all-purpose flour

½ teaspoon baking powder

½ teaspoon kosher salt

1 cup milk

2 tablespoons butter, melted

2 eggs, separated

2 cups corn kernels
(from about 3 ears corn)

2 green onions, thinly sliced

Canola oil, for frying

Flaky salt, such as Maldon,
for serving

WHEN I WAS A KID, it wasn't uncommon for our family of five to finish off twelve or fifteen ears of corn at dinner in August, when the locally grown stuff started showing up at Vermont farm stands, three bucks a dozen. We'd lay those boiled ears on cold sticks of butter, roll them to coat, then devour them end to end, typewriter-style.

I still think that's the best way to eat summer corn (greedily), but these crispy, light fritters are a close second. Shallow-fried until golden brown, the pancakes puff and the edges get irresistibly crunchy. You can add cheese or herbs to the batter; you can serve them for breakfast with a puddle of maple syrup, for lunch with some dressed arugula alongside, or with dinner as a side dish. Any leftover fritters can be reheated on a wire rack set over a baking sheet in a hot oven.

> In a large bowl, whisk together the flour, baking powder, and salt. Create a well in the center of the flour and pour in the milk, melted butter, and egg yolks. Whisk until smooth, then cover and refrigerate for an hour.

> Remove the batter from the refrigerator and stir in the corn kernels and green onions.

> Put the egg whites in the bowl of an electric mixer fitted with the whisk attachment (or put them in a bowl and get a large whisk) and beat until they hold soft peaks. Fold the egg whites into the corn mixture until no streaks of white are visible.

> Set a wire cooling rack over a rimmed baking sheet and preheat the oven to 250°F. Pour ½ inch of canola oil into a heavy high-sided frying pan. Heat over medium heat until the oil is hot; if you add a drop of water to the oil, it should sizzle vigorously. Without crowding the pan, scoop quarter-cup mounds of fritter batter into the hot oil and fry, turning once, until the fritters are golden brown on both sides, about 4 to 5 minutes. Don't get all rushy-rushy here and turn up the heat. If the oil gets too hot, they'll darken on the exterior before they're cooked inside—and also, the corn can start to pop!

> Use a spatula to transfer the fritters to the cooling rack and place in the oven to keep warm. Skim any corn kernels from the oil with a slotted spoon, then fry the remaining batter in batches until all the batter has been used, transferring each batch of finished fritters to the oven to keep warm.

> Arrange the fritters on a large platter and season with flaky salt. Serve hot.

Roasted Carrots *with* Burrata *and* Salsa Rustica

Serves 4 to 6

2 bunches small carrots
(about 16)

½ cup plus 2 tablespoons
extra-virgin olive oil

1 cup packed parsley leaves,
finely chopped

½ cup packed mint leaves,
finely chopped

¼ cup roasted salted pistachios,
coarsely chopped

2 tablespoons minced shallots

2 teaspoons lemon juice

1 teaspoon lemon zest

Kosher salt

Freshly ground black pepper

2 (8-ounce) balls burrata

Flaky salt, such as Maldon,
for serving

I AM NOT ORDINARILY the kind of cranky person who orders something at a restaurant and then grouses about how she could make it at home, but I've got to admit that every time I order a burrata (which is often; I haven't learned my lesson), I become one.

That's because by purchasing a ball of burrata, you're 90 percent of the way to a starter you'd pay fourteen dollars for in a restaurant. Burrata, a mozzarella-like cow's-milk cheese that has been formed into a pouch and filled with curds and cream, is luscious, rich, and milky. It's great with juicy ripe tomatoes; actually, there's hardly a vegetable that isn't great with burrata.

This recipe works best with smallish carrots, about three-quarters of an inch thick. I roast them whole until tender and blackened in spots, coaxing out their natural sweetness, then top them with the cheese and salsa rustica, a zippy, acidic herb sauce enriched with pistachios. Because I like to go all out, I recommend two balls of burrata, but you could exercise slightly more restraint (and lower your grocery bill) by making do with one.

> Preheat the oven to 450°F. Toss the carrots with 2 tablespoons of the olive oil and spread on a rimmed baking sheet or in a large cast-iron pan. Bake, shaking the pan occasionally, until the carrots are tender and blackened in spots, about 45 minutes. (Use your judgment here; if you've got tiny carrots, they won't take as long to roast.) Let the carrots cool slightly, then transfer to a platter.

> While the carrots roast, make the salsa rustica: In a bowl, combine the chopped herbs, pistachios, shallots, lemon juice and zest, and the remaining ½ cup olive oil. Season to taste with salt and pepper.

> To serve, use your hands to tear each burrata into large pieces, then set on top of the carrots and spoon the salsa rustica over. Top with a little flaky salt.

Chicory Salad *with* Maple-Roasted Squash *and* Blue Cheese

Serves 6

½ cup pumpkin seeds

Kosher salt

1 medium delicata squash, peeled, seeded, halved, and cut crosswise into ¼-inch-thick slices

1 medium red onion, peeled and cut into 8 wedges

¼ cup plus 3 tablespoons extra-virgin olive oil

Freshly ground black pepper

2 tablespoons maple syrup

1 teaspoon grainy Dijon mustard

3 tablespoons red wine or sherry vinegar

8 cups mixed chicories, washed, dried, and torn into bite-size pieces

½ cup crumbled blue cheese

I N WINTER, my body longs for something crunchy and refreshing to combat the rich braises and other stick-to-your-ribs foods my lizard brain demands when it's cold.

In this salad, the bitterness of the chicories—which take many forms, from frilly frisée to bitter, deep fuchsia radicchio—is countered by maple-roasted squash and red onion, whose sweetness is in turn balanced by the blue cheese. A final sprinkling of toasted pumpkin seeds adds crunch.

If yours is the kind of family that allows new additions to the Thanksgiving table from year to year, consider making this salad part of the feast.

———

> Preheat the oven to 350°F. Spread the pumpkin seeds in a small cast-iron frying pan or on a rimmed baking sheet, transfer to the oven, and bake until lightly toasted, about 6 minutes. Remove from the oven and season the seeds with a pinch of salt.

> Put the sliced squash and onion wedges in a large bowl, drizzle with 3 tablespoons of the olive oil, and season with salt and pepper. Transfer to a rimmed baking sheet, spread in a single layer, and bake, turning once, until the squash is tender and golden brown on both sides and the onion wedges are soft and slightly frizzled, about 25 to 30 minutes. Drizzle with the maple syrup and bake 5 minutes more, until the squash and onions are lightly caramelized. Remove from the oven and let cool. The squash and onions can be roasted in advance and refrigerated; bring to room temperature before using.

> While the squash roasts, make the dressing: In a small bowl whisk together the mustard, a pinch of salt and some pepper, and the vinegar. Whisk in the remaining ¼ cup of olive oil and continue whisking until the dressing is emulsified.

> Put the chicories in a large salad bowl. Add the roasted squash and onions, the blue cheese, and the pumpkin seeds, pour the dressing over, and toss gently with your hands to combine. Season with additional salt and pepper and serve.

Avocado *and* Citrus Salad *with* Shallot Vinaigrette

Serves 4

1 small shallot, peeled and minced (about 2 tablespoons)

½ teaspoon Dijon mustard

2 tablespoons lemon juice

¼ cup extra-virgin olive oil

Kosher salt and freshly ground black pepper

2 avocados, halved and pitted

1 large navel or Cara Cara orange

1 blood orange

1 grapefruit (white or pink)

3 tangerines or mandarins

Flaky salt, such as Maldon, for serving

THE COMBINATION of avocado and citrus isn't particularly novel, but that doesn't keep it from being welcome in the winter. Though the salad is dead simple to make, its success relies on a nice assortment of citrus. You want a combination of sweet and tart varieties; beyond that, the specifics are unimportant. Choose avocados that yield to slight pressure at the stem end; if you're unsure about their ripeness (selecting ripe avocados is not a strength of mine), buy one or two more than you need as an insurance policy.

Cutting the avocados and citrus into different shapes isn't essential, but it does prevent the salad from looking too flat on the plate. (God is in the details! Or so they say.) If you can find Meyer lemons, use their juice in the vinaigrette.

> In a small bowl, whisk together the shallot, mustard, and lemon juice and let stand 10 minutes, which will mellow the harshness of the raw shallot. Whisk in the olive oil and continue whisking until the dressing is emulsified, then season to taste with salt and pepper. Set aside.

> Cut each avocado half lengthwise into thirds, then cut each avocado baton in half diagonally and peel each piece. With a sharp knife, cut the ends off the oranges and the grapefruit. Working with one piece of fruit at a time, use a sharp knife to cut off the peel and pith, following the curve of the fruit. Cut the oranges into wagon wheels and transfer to a bowl. With a sharp knife, cut each grapefruit segment free of its membrane and add it to the bowl with the oranges. Squeeze the grapefruit shell over the bowl to collect the juice. Peel the tangerines, separate the segments, and add them to the bowl with the other citrus. Toss gently to combine.

> Arrange the fruit on a platter and add the avocado pieces, tucking them in and around the fruit. Spoon the shallot vinaigrette over and season with a flaky salt and pepper. Serve immediately.

Creamy Onion Tart *with* Olives

Makes one 12-inch tart

FOR THE CRUST:

5 tablespoons cold unsalted butter, cut into small cubes

1½ cups all-purpose flour

¼ teaspoon kosher salt

3 tablespoons vegetable shortening, lard, or cold bacon fat

1 large egg

2 to 3 tablespoons ice water

FOR THE TART:

4 tablespoons unsalted butter

3 large white onions, peeled and thinly sliced

¼ teaspoon sugar

Kosher salt and freshly ground black pepper

½ cup heavy cream

1 egg

2 anchovy fillets

1 clove garlic, peeled

½ cup olives, black or green, pitted and chopped

1 teaspoon thyme leaves, chopped

3 tablespoons extra-virgin olive oil

I KNOW A WOMAN who never cooks the same thing twice for guests. She keeps a journal noting when and to whom she served each particular dish, ensuring there are never any repeats. I'm sort of in awe of her record-keeping, especially since I can't recall what I ate for breakfast by the time dinner rolls around, but her method is antithetical to my own; I believe in repeats, in making a dish so often and for so many people that it becomes inextricably linked to you, something friends request and look forward to eating or want the recipe for. Your culinary calling card, so to speak.

My friend Nan Duffly believes in repeats too, and every year around the holidays, she hosts an open house at which she serves the same dishes, including a spiced, cured beef tenderloin, cooked rare and sliced thin, and a version of this exceptional onion tart.

The recipe was originally published in the *Boston Globe;* Nan adapted it slightly and I have adapted it a bit more, adding a briny olive topping that complements the sweet onions and flaky pastry, but it's awesome even without that flourish. It has enough custard to bind it but not so much that it detracts from the onions. I like the mellow sweetness of white onions in this recipe, but you can substitute yellow instead.

Adding a bit of shortening to the pastry makes it especially flaky (come at me, haters), but you could use all butter or substitute lard or bacon fat for the shortening.

> **FOR THE CRUST:** Spread the cubed butter in a small dish in a single layer and freeze until very cold, 15 minutes. In a food processor, pulse the flour and salt until blended. Add butter and shortening and pulse until the butter chunks are about the size of peas. In a small bowl, lightly beat the egg and 2 tablespoons of the ice water. Add the egg mixture to the food processor and

RECIPE CONTINUES ⬊

pulse just until the mixture holds together in a shaggy ball (you may need to add the additional tablespoon water).

> Turn the dough out onto a sheet of plastic wrap, use the plastic wrap to gather the dough into a ball, then flatten it into a disk with the heel of your hand. Tightly wrap and chill at least 1 hour and up to 3 days. (The dough can be frozen for up to a month. Let thaw overnight in the refrigerator before using.)

> **FOR THE FILLING**: In a large frying pan, heat the butter over medium heat until it melts. Add the sliced onions and sugar and cook, stirring occasionally, until all the liquid has evaporated, about 15 to 20 minutes. The onions should be soft and light golden brown. Season to taste with salt and pepper. Remove from the heat, transfer to a bowl, and let cool. In a small bowl, whisk together the cream and egg. When the onions are cool, add the cream mixture and stir to combine.

> Preheat the oven to 400°F. Remove the dough from the refrigerator and let stand 5 minutes. Unwrap and, on a lightly floured surface with a lightly floured rolling pin, roll dough into a 14-inch circle. Use a paring knife to trim the shaggy edges. Transfer to a parchment-lined baking sheet. Top with the onion mixture, spreading in an even layer and leaving a 1½-inch border. Fold the border over and pleat and crimp to create a crust. (If you're making this tart for stand-up eating, roll the dough into a large rectangle instead of a circle, and cut it into squares after it's baked.) Transfer to the oven and bake until the crust is a deep golden brown, about 45 minutes. Remove from the oven and let cool.

> In a mortar and pestle, pound the anchovy fillets and garlic to a paste (if you don't have a mortar and pestle, you can finely mince the anchovies and garlic and then use the side of your knife to grind into a paste). Transfer to a bowl and stir in the olives, thyme leaves, and olive oil. Dot the olive mixture evenly over the surface of the tart, then cut it into wedges and serve.

Seeded Rye Gougères

Makes 2 dozen

1 cup milk or water

8 tablespoons butter

¾ teaspoon kosher salt

⅔ cup all-purpose flour

⅓ cup rye flour

4 eggs

1 cup grated Gruyère cheese

FOR THE TOPPING:

1 egg

½ teaspoon kosher salt

2 teaspoons sesame seeds

2 teaspoons sunflower seeds

1 teaspoon poppy seeds

WHEN I WORKED AT LA VARENNE, the French cooking school in Burgundy, I always volunteered to go on the morning bakery run; I drove the beat-up school car to the village boulangerie for baguettes and bought a cheesy gougère for the ride home. Lyle Lovett's album *Pontiac* was stuck in the car's tape deck, so that became the unlikely sound track of that summer.

While in Burgundy, I learned how to make veal demi-glace and pike quenelles and *pâte feuilletée.* But of all of the French recipes I picked up, it's choux (pronounced "shoe") pastry I make the most. This simple dough, used for gougères (and éclairs), is easy to make and totally rewarding. I love to watch them inflate in the oven into airy, rich puffs.

I like to add a bit of rye flour to this and other savory doughs (you'll notice I include some in the dough for my calzones, page 121), just enough to impart a nutty flavor that is enhanced by the Gruyère and the seeded topping. It's completely optional, though, and the gougères will be equally good if made entirely with all-purpose flour.

If you want to make a sweet version, omit the cheese and seeded topping. Once cooled, split them, fill them with scoops of ice cream, and serve with chocolate or caramel sauce drizzled over.

> Preheat the oven to 425°F. Combine the milk, butter, and salt in a medium-size, heavy-bottomed saucepan. Bring to a boil over medium heat, then reduce the heat to medium low and add the flours all at once. Cook, stirring, until the mixture comes together into a ball and begins to leave a film on the bottom of the pan, 2 to 3 minutes.

> Transfer the dough to the bowl of an electric mixer fitted with the paddle attachment. Mix the dough on low speed to cool it slightly. When steam is no longer rising from the dough, add the eggs one at a time, mixing each egg in completely before adding the next. Fold in all but 2 tablespoons of the cheese and transfer the dough to a piping bag. (Alternatively, you can forget the piping bag

RECIPE CONTINUES ↘

and just scoop the dough onto the baking sheet with a spoon.)

> Line two rimmed baking sheets with silicone baking mats or parchment paper. Snip the end off the piping bag with a pair of scissors and pipe the dough onto the prepared pans in 1½-inch mounds, spacing them about 2 inches apart. Wet your fingertip and smooth the tops of each mound.

> MAKE THE TOPPING: In a small bowl, beat together the egg and salt. In a second small bowl, stir together the sesame, sunflower, and poppy seeds. With a pastry brush, brush each gougère with some of the egg wash, then top each with some of the seed mixture and some of the reserved grated cheese.

> Transfer the pans to the oven and bake until the gougères are puffed and deep golden brown, about 24 minutes. Do not underbake or the gougères will collapse when they're pulled out of the oven. Remove from the oven and, with a skewer or toothpick, poke a hole in the side of each gougère (this allows the steam within to escape and prevents them from deflating). Serve warm.

> Gougères can be made ahead and frozen. I pipe the dough onto lined pans and freeze it, then transfer the frozen unbaked gougères to a plastic freezer storage bag, and freeze for up to 2 months. They can be baked from frozen, though you may need to add a few minutes in the oven. Baked gougères can also be frozen; let them cool completely, then transfer to a plastic freezer storage bag and freeze for up to 1 month. Reheat in a 400°F oven until hot, about 8 minutes.

Pretzel Rolls

Makes 16 rolls

4½ cups all-purpose flour

1¾ cups water

¼ cup nonfat dry milk (if you don't have this, replace 1 cup of the water in the recipe with whole milk)

2 tablespoons unsalted butter, softened

2 teaspoons instant dry yeast

1 teaspoon kosher salt

¼ cup food-grade lye

Pretzel salt, for topping

MOST COMMERCIALLY AVAILABLE soft pretzels, like the ones you get off carts in New York City or in the mall, are garbage, soft, flavorless twists that are often slicked with artificial-butter-flavored oil. But in Germany and Switzerland, excellent pretzels are ubiquitous and delicious, with burnished salt-speckled exteriors that give way to plush interiors. You can get them plain or split and topped with ham, cheese, butter, smoked fish—you name it. Forget the watches and the trains that are always on time; if you want proof that Switzerland is a highly evolved country, just look to those pretzels.

To make a pretzel roll that really tastes like a pretzel, however, you have to be willing to don some safety goggles and rubber gloves. Dipping the dough in a mixture of water and food-grade lye is what gives pretzels their color and signature flavor, but you have to be careful with lye, which is a harsh chemical. Food-grade lye can be ordered online, but if you prefer to avoid lye altogether, you can make a decent pretzel by dipping the dough in a baking-soda bath instead. I've given instructions for that on the facing page, though I will say that in a side-by-side taste test, the lye pretzels handily bested their baking-soda brethren.

Eat them plain or split them and stuff with whatever you like: butter and ham; salami, cheddar, and mustard; or a stinky cheese like Taleggio with a spoonful of fruit chutney.

These pretzels are best eaten the same day they're made; they get soggy when they sit. If you're storing them overnight, put them in a paper bag rather than plastic, then warm them in a hot oven to recrisp before serving. Though I've given instructions for rolls, the dough can also be shaped into the traditional pretzel form, if you prefer.

> In a medium bowl, combine the flour, water, nonfat dry milk, butter, yeast, and salt and mix with a wooden spoon until a rough dough forms. Transfer to a lightly floured work surface and knead into a smooth ball. Transfer to a lightly greased bowl, cover, and let rise in a warm place until doubled, about an hour.

> Lightly grease a rimmed baking sheet and line a second baking sheet with parchment paper. Preheat the oven to 400°F. Turn the dough out onto an unfloured work

surface and divide into 16 pieces, about 2 ounces each. Working with one piece at a time, cup your hand over the dough, letting your palm rest gently on the dough and your fingers form a cage around it. Apply some light pressure to the dough while simultaneously rotating your hand clockwise. The dough should catch on the work surface and tighten into a smooth ball. Transfer to the baking sheet and repeat with the remaining dough until all the rolls have been formed. Cover with a clean kitchen towel and let rest 15 minutes.

> Line a baking sheet with a silicone baking mat and don your safety goggles and rubber gloves. Place a large glass or plastic bowl in the sink and add 1 quart cold water. Slowly stir in the lye, taking care not to splash it on your skin or in the sink. Transfer a few rolls at a time into the water, turning them so both sides get wet, then transfer to the prepared baking sheet. Discard the lye water by pouring it down the drain (lye is often used to unclog drains, so you're getting a two-for-one here). Using scissors or a sharp knife, cut a ¼-inch-deep X

into the center of each bun. Sprinkle with pretzel salt.

> Bake for 20 to 24 minutes, until dark brown. Remove from the oven and transfer to a rack to cool. The pretzel rolls are best eaten the day they're made. If storing them overnight, place in a paper bag (plastic will cause the salt to melt) and warm in a low oven before serving to recrisp.

___

Note · For the baking-soda bath: In a large saucepan, combine 4 cups water, 2 tablespoons baking soda, and 1½ teaspoons kosher salt. Bring to a simmer, then add a few rolls to the water, turning with a spoon so both sides get wet. With a slotted spoon, remove the rolls from the water and transfer to the parchment-lined baking sheet. Cut, top with salt, and bake as described at left.

Fried Salt-and-Pepper Shrimp

Serves 4 to 6

1½ pounds medium or large shell-on shrimp, preferably Gulf shrimp

1 teaspoon sugar

¼ teaspoon Sichuan peppercorns, toasted and ground

¼ teaspoon white peppercorns, toasted and ground

½ teaspoon kosher salt

Canola oil, for frying

½ cup cornstarch

1 jalapeño chile, thinly sliced into rings

¼ cup cilantro leaves

HAVE PROBABLY BURNED the roof of my mouth half a dozen times eating salt-and-pepper shrimp at my favorite Chinese restaurant; I can never wait until they cool to scarf them down.

This recipe calls for shell-on shrimp; the frying makes the shells crispy and entirely edible, and that texture is part of what makes them irresistible. Don't worry if your shrimp have been previously frozen; most have been, and they freeze quite well (although if you can find fresh shell-on Gulf shrimp—lucky you—by all means, use them). You should, however, be very wary of shrimp that have been rinsed with chlorine solution (a practice that's legal but compromises their flavor) or shrimp that have been treated with preservatives. The size of the shrimp doesn't matter tremendously for this recipe, but I usually select medium or large, as I think the shrimp labeled *jumbo* are often tougher.

I use a combination of floral Sichuan peppercorns and white peppercorns; the fried jalapeño rings add another layer of heat.

———

> With a sharp pair of scissors, cut through the shell along the back of each shrimp to reveal the vein; devein the shrimp by pulling out the vein with the tip of a sharp knife (if the shrimp still have heads, cut them off using the scissors). In a small bowl, mix together the sugar, ground peppercorns, and salt.

> Heat 3 inches of canola oil in a heavy, high-sided pot over high heat. Put the cornstarch in a large bowl. Line a second large bowl with paper towels and set nearby. Working with a third of the shrimp at a time, dredge the shrimp in the cornstarch, turning to coat on all sides. When the oil registers 375°F on a deep-frying thermometer, add the shrimp and fry until crispy and bright pink, about 3 minutes. With a spider or slotted spoon, transfer the shrimp from the oil to the paper-towel-lined bowl.

> Repeat the dredging and frying with the remaining shrimp, cooking them in two batches and letting the oil return to temperature between each batch. As each batch of shrimp is cooked, transfer them to the bowl with the others.

RECIPE CONTINUES ꜱ

> When all of the shrimp have been fried, add the chile slices to the oil and fry for 10 seconds. Remove from the oil with a spider or slotted spoon and transfer to the bowl with the shrimp. Remove the paper towels from the bowl. Season the shrimp generously with the salt-and-pepper mixture, tossing the shrimp so they are coated on all sides. Add the cilantro leaves and toss again to combine. Serve immediately.

Cheater's Tortilla Española

Makes one 9-inch tortilla

1 pound Yukon Gold potatoes

1 cup extra-virgin olive oil

1 small yellow onion, peeled and thinly sliced

10 eggs

Kosher salt and freshly ground pepper

Flaky salt, such as Maldon, for serving

Aioli (page 35) or Fancy Mayonnaise (page 62), for serving

TORTILLA ESPAÑOLA has a lot to recommend it. The Spanish savory cake is made with basic ingredients (including my desert-island duo, eggs and potatoes), it can be served warm or cold, and it's a nice vehicle for a generous slather of aioli.

Most recipes for tortillas suggest that you flip it midway through cooking—indeed, traditionalists will tell you that this step is part of what makes a tortilla a tortilla. But I've always found that step to be sort of high stakes and messy (as in, I've flipped one right onto the burner of the stove; the smell of charred egg haunting me for days), and the resulting tortilla is no better than the one I make using a different method.

When I make a tortilla, I cook it until it's set on the bottom, then pop it under the broiler to brown and set the top. No flipping required. It may not be traditional, but you won't care about tradition if your tortilla ends up on the floor, right? My nouveau technique requires you to use a pan that can go from stovetop to broiler.

Leftover tortilla wedges make a great sandwich filling.

———

> With a mandoline or sharp knife, slice the potatoes into ¼-inch-thick coins. Heat the olive oil in a 9-inch cast-iron frying pan over medium heat. Add the potatoes and onion and stir gently, then push down beneath the oil (the pan will be a bit crowded at first, but as the onions cook, the volume will decrease). Reduce the heat so the oil is bubbling gently and cook until the potatoes and onions are tender but not browned, about 10 minutes. Drain into a colander set over a heatproof bowl and reserve the oil.

> In a large bowl, beat the eggs until well mixed. Season generously with salt and pepper and gently stir in the potato-onion mixture. In the same frying pan you used to cook the potatoes and onions, heat 1 tablespoon of the reserved oil over medium heat. Arrange an oven rack about 3 inches from the broiler and preheat the broiler.

> Pour the egg-potato mixture into the frying pan, reduce the heat to medium low, and cook until the edges of the tortilla

RECIPE CONTINUES ⭦

are set and the underside is golden brown (peek to ensure the bottom isn't browning too quickly), about 5 minutes, periodically running a rubber spatula around the inner edges of the pan to prevent the eggs from sticking; the top will still be runny.

> Transfer the pan to the oven and broil until the top

is puffed, golden brown, and set, about 3 minutes. Remove from the oven and run the spatula around the inner edges of the pan to loosen the tortilla. Invert a large plate over the pan and, in one motion, flip the pan over so the tortilla is on the plate. Let cool slightly, then sprinkle with flaky salt and serve with aioli or Fancy Mayonnaise.

Fancy Mayonnaise

> If I've not yet convinced you to make your own aioli or if you're too pressed for time to do it, there's no shame in gussying up some store-bought mayonnaise. I was raised in the church of Hellmann's (called Best Foods out west), so that's what I prefer. I enhance it with a squeeze of lemon juice and garlic paste (garlic pounded with a pinch of salt) to taste. You can add chopped herbs if you like, or some pesto or a spoonful of harissa (page 82).

Scottish Oatcakes *with* Butter *and* Dates

Makes 3 dozen oatcakes

1 cup rolled oats

1 cup whole-wheat flour

½ cup oat bran

⅓ cup packed light brown sugar

½ teaspoon baking soda

¼ teaspoon fine sea salt

8 tablespoons cold unsalted butter, cubed

¼ cup water

Salted butter (preferably Kerrygold), at room temperature, *or* soft blue cheese (such as Saint Agur), at room temperature, for serving

Pitted Medjool dates, quartered, for serving

MY GRANDMOTHER JESSIE, my namesake, came to live with us when I was thirteen. Born and raised in Nova Scotia, of Scottish descent, she was a wonderful person but a bad cook—I got neither my enthusiasm for cooking nor any recipes from her. The one good thing I do remember her baking was oatcakes. She never wrote down the recipe, so I had to reverse-engineer it from memory.

These oatcakes are gently sweet, more cracker than cookie, but it's that sweetness that makes them excellent topped with creamy blue cheese or a slather of good salted Irish butter. If you care to gild the lily, a sliver of Medjool date on top of either cheese or butter does the trick.

―――

> Preheat the oven to 350°F. Combine the oats, flour, oat bran, brown sugar, baking soda, and sea salt in a bowl. Add the cubed butter and work the butter into the flour mixture with your fingertips or a pastry cutter until the butter is in pea-size pieces. Pour in the water and stir until a crumbly dough forms. Turn out onto a lightly floured work surface and use your hands to compact the dough into a ball.

> With a lightly floured rolling pin, roll the dough to a thickness of ¼ inch. Cut the dough into rounds with a 2-inch round cutter and transfer to unlined baking sheets, spacing them about half an inch apart (they do not spread). Roll out scraps and repeat.

> Bake the oatcakes until golden brown on the edges, about 13 minutes. Let cool on the pan. The oatcakes will keep in an airtight container for up to a week or can be frozen for up to a month.

> To serve, spread each oatcake with some of the butter or blue cheese and top with a date quarter.

Twice-Baked Magic Soufflés

Makes 6 soufflés

5 tablespoons unsalted butter

½ cup finely chopped leeks

¼ cup all-purpose flour

1½ cups whole milk, warmed

1 teaspoon kosher salt

Pinch of ground nutmeg

1½ cups grated Parmigiano-Reggiano

1 cup heavy cream

5 eggs, separated

SOUFFLÉS HAVE ACQUIRED a reputation as temperamental and difficult, but they were once part of the repertoire of every home cook; Julia Child included sixteen pages of soufflé techniques and recipes in *Mastering the Art of French Cooking*. In reality, if you can whip an egg white you can make a soufflé, and they are far less fragile than you might think.

The challenge lies not in technique but in timing, because once a soufflé is pulled from a hot oven, it begins to deflate. One easy work-around is to bake the soufflés twice, a trick I learned from Anne Willan at La Varenne; it liberates the cook from the high-stakes moment of pulling a soufflé from the oven and serving it before it deflates.

The individual soufflés are baked once, turned out of the ramekins into a baking dish, coated with cream sauce and cheese, then baked—up to twenty-four hours later!—a second time. They puff up again, as forgiving as can be. Magic!

―――

> Preheat the oven to 425°F and generously grease six 8-ounce ramekins. In a medium saucepan over medium-low heat, melt 1 tablespoon of the butter. Add the leeks and cook, stirring, until soft but not brown, 4 to 5 minutes. Transfer to a bowl and set aside.

> Melt the remaining 4 tablespoons of butter over medium heat in the same saucepan that you used for the leeks. When the butter stops foaming, whisk in the flour and cook, whisking, for 1 minute. Whisk in the milk and cook, whisking, until the mixture boils and thickens. Stir in the salt, nutmeg, 1¼ cups of the cheese, and the leeks. Transfer a third of the mixture to a bowl, whisk in the cream, and set aside. Whisk the egg yolks into the remaining two-thirds, then transfer the mixture to a large bowl.

> In the bowl of an electric mixer fitted with a whisk attachment (or in a large bowl with a handheld mixer), beat the egg whites with a pinch of salt until they hold stiff peaks. Stir a third of the whites into the yolk mixture

RECIPE CONTINUES ↘

to lighten it, then fold in the remaining two-thirds until no streaks of white remain. Divide the mixture among the greased ramekins, smooth the tops, then run the tip of your finger around the inner edge of each ramekin (this will help the soufflé rise higher and straighter). Arrange the ramekins in a baking dish and pour enough hot water into the baking dish to come half an inch up the side of the ramekins.

> Transfer to the oven and bake until puffed, deep golden brown, and set within, about 25 minutes. Remove from the oven, remove the ramekins from the water bath, and let the soufflés cool (they will deflate).

> Run a knife around the inner edge of each ramekin, then turn the soufflés out into a gratin dish and pour the reserved cream mixture over and around the soufflés. Top each with some of the reserved Parmigiano. At this point, the soufflés can be covered with plastic wrap and refrigerated for up to 24 hours (I'm telling you, this recipe is magic).

> When you're ready to bake the soufflés a second time, preheat the oven to 425°F. Bake until the soufflés are puffed and browned (they will puff as much as—if not more than—the first time they were baked), about 10 to 15 minutes. Serve immediately.

Duck Rillettes

Makes about 4 cups

3 tablespoons kosher salt

1 teaspoon freshly ground black pepper

2 bay leaves, broken into pieces

4 whole duck legs

3 sprigs fresh thyme

3 pounds (6½ cups) duck fat

Crackers or toasts, for serving

Grainy mustard, for serving

Cornichon pickles, for serving

F YOU'RE WARY OF COOKING DUCK, consider rillettes your gateway drug. To make this spreadable pâté, duck legs are first cured with salt and spices, then submerged in duck fat and slowly cooked until the meat is silky and tender. You could stop there—confit duck legs can be carefully removed from the fat, seared, skin-side down, until the skin is crispy and the meat is warmed through, then served as a main course.

Or you can take one more small but worthy step and pull the confit meat from the bones, shred it, and combine it with pan juices and some of its cooking fat to make rillettes. What a snack! I like it best spread thick on toasted bread, maybe with a swipe of grainy mustard or a cornichon pickle on top.

Though this takes a few days to make, both the confit and the rillettes will keep, refrigerated, for up to 1 month.

> In a small bowl, stir together the salt, pepper, and bay leaves. Arrange the duck legs in a rimmed baking dish large enough to accommodate them in a single layer and season on both sides with the salt mixture, using all of it. Tuck the sprigs of thyme around the duck. Loosely cover with plastic wrap and refrigerate for at least 24 hours and up to 2 days. Remove the duck from the fridge, discard the thyme, rinse the legs under cold water, and set on a paper-towel-lined plate.

> Preheat the oven to 200°F. Melt the duck fat in a large Dutch oven over low heat. Slip the duck legs into the melted fat (they should be completely submerged), cover the pot, and transfer to the oven. Cook until the duck is very tender and beginning to fall from the bone, about 2 to 2½ hours. Remove from the oven and carefully, with a slotted spoon, transfer the duck legs to a plate.

> Let the fat cool to room temperature, then ladle it through a fine-mesh sieve into glass mason jars or other freezer-safe storage containers (quart-size yogurt containers are particularly handy), taking care not to disturb the pan juices that have sunk to the bottom of the pot.

> Remove and discard the skin and bones from the duck

RECIPE CONTINUES ↘

and shred the meat. Transfer the meat to the bowl of an electric mixer fitted with the paddle attachment.

> Add ¼ cup of the pan juices from the bottom of the pan and mix on low speed. (Reserve the remaining juices, which are packed with ducky flavor; they will solidify once chilled and can be added to soups, beans, or pan sauces to boost flavor. If you don't have an immediate use for the juices, they can also be frozen.) Add a few tablespoons of the duck fat and mix on low speed to combine. It's possible to overmix, so exercise some caution; the mixture should be almost spreadable but the meat fibers shouldn't be so broken down that it's paste-like. Taste—it should be juicy and well seasoned. Add additional pan juices, fat, or salt as needed.

> Pack the rillettes firmly into two wide-mouth pint jars, smoothing the top and leaving about an inch of space at the top of each jar. Set the jars on a rimmed baking sheet and carefully spoon or pour some of the reserved fat into each jar; the fat should completely cover the meat (if any of the meat is exposed to air, it will spoil, so make sure it's covered with a thick layer of fat). The remaining duck fat can be refrigerated for up to a month or frozen for up to six; it can be used for multiple batches of duck confit or as a cooking medium for the world's best roasted potatoes.

> Cover the jars and transfer to the refrigerator. Duck rillettes will keep, refrigerated, for up to a month. To serve, let the rillettes come to room temperature. Serve with crackers or toasts (page 36), accompanied by grainy mustard and cornichon pickles.

Ultra-Crispy Potato Pancakes

Makes about 15 pancakes

3 pounds Yukon Gold potatoes

3 eggs, lightly beaten

½ cup dry bread crumbs or matzo meal

1 tablespoon kosher salt

1 teaspoon ground black pepper

3 cups canola oil

Flaky salt, for serving

Crème fraîche (page 221) or sour cream, for serving (optional)

IT SORT OF MAKES ME MAD, all the terrible potato pancakes I've eaten in my life. For something so simple, they seem to prove vexing to many cooks, and I've had my fair share of soggy, greasy, floppy latkes. I didn't grow up making or eating these, so I'm not hidebound by tradition or family recipe, meaning I make them just how I like them, really crunchy on the exterior with a creamy, tender interior.

Two keys to crispness: You must extract the maximum amount of liquid from the grated potatoes, and you must fry them in a good quantity of hot oil. Neutral canola oil is usually my choice, though if you happen to have some duck fat sitting around (left over from the Duck Rillettes on page 69, maybe?), you could use half duck fat, half oil for an especially righteous, deeply savory pancake.

Serving potato pancakes with applesauce has never really made sense to me. I like crème fraîche or sour cream instead, and I'm not above swiping them through a puddle of ketchup. If you make the pancakes a bit smaller, they're nice little hors d'oeuvres—you could top them with some crème fraîche and smoked salmon or that caviar you have lying around. You could serve them as a side dish along with eggs or grilled sausages or braised beef; accompanied by a big salad, they can be the centerpiece of a meal.

———

> Peel the potatoes and coarsely grate with a box grater or the grater attachment on a food processor. Transfer the grated potatoes to a large bowl and add cold water to cover. Let stand 15 minutes. Put handfuls of grated potato into a ricer and squeeze to remove all the moisture (if you don't have a ricer, you can wrap handfuls of grated potatoes in a clean kitchen towel and squeeze to extract the liquid). Really give it your all—soggy potatoes make soggy potato pancakes. Transfer the potatoes to a clean bowl and add the eggs, bread crumbs, kosher salt, and black pepper and mix to combine.

> Pour ¾ inch of oil into a high-sided 10-inch frying pan (a cast-iron one works well), line a plate with paper towels, and set a wire rack over a rimmed baking sheet. Preheat the oven to 250°F. Heat the

oil until it registers 350°F on a deep-frying thermometer. (If you don't have a deep-frying thermometer, stick the end of a wooden chopstick into the oil. If tiny bubbles appear, it's the right temperature.) Scoop up a scant ½ cup of the potato mixture and use your hands to form it into a disk about ½ inch thick and 2½ inches wide. Place the formed pancake onto a spatula and carefully slide it into the hot oil. Form four more pancakes the same way, and add them to the pan. Fry the pancakes until dark golden brown and crispy on their undersides, about 4 minutes, then flip and fry on the second side until dark golden brown, 3 to 4 minutes longer. Remove from the oil, place on the paper-towel-lined plate to drain, then transfer to the wire rack. Place the wire rack (with baking sheet beneath) in the oven to keep the pancakes warm while you fry the rest.

> Use a fine-mesh strainer or slotted spoon to scoop out any bits of potato in the pan and let the oil return to temperature. You might notice that as time goes by, liquid will start to accumulate in the bowl containing the potatoes. Tilting the bowl slightly will allow the liquid to accumulate on one side, and you can move the potatoes to the opposite side, away from any lake that forms, and drain off the liquid as necessary. As I make my second and third batches of pancakes, I give each handful of grated potatoes a squeeze to eliminate as much liquid as possible before forming them into cakes. Continue frying the pancakes in batches of five as described above, transferring the cooked pancakes to the oven to keep warm.

> Just before serving, transfer the pancakes to a plate and shower with flaky salt. Serve warm, with crème fraîche alongside, if using.

Negronis *and* Potato Chips

Makes 1 Negroni

1½ ounces dry gin
(I like Beefeater)

1 ounce Campari

1 ounce sweet vermouth

Orange twist, for garnish

1 bag plain potato chips
(no need to get fancy here;
Lay's will do)

I HAVE NEVER MET A PERSON who does not like potato chips, but it didn't occur to me that they had a place in the entertaining canon beyond Super Bowl parties until I went to Rome. There, when the sun starts to dip low, visitors and locals alike nab tables at bars overlooking a piazza. While the kids chase pigeons, the adults drink Negronis and eat bowls of complimentary snacks—usually Castelvetrano olives, maybe some salty roasted peanuts, and always, always, a little bowl of potato chips. If it's good enough for the Italians, it's good enough for me, and since then I've adopted the tradition. Not surprisingly, no matter what snacks I put out alongside the chips, the chips are always the first to go.

Though I've memorized dozens of recipes in my life, I have a difficult time remembering how to make most cocktails. But the three-ingredient Negroni is easy to master, and the drink's bitterness piques the appetite, making it the ideal predinner cocktail. The combination of salty potato chips and an ice-cold Negroni is one of the better ones out there. Because a Negroni is made entirely of spirit, it can easily be batched to serve a crowd (or, you know, yourself) and refrigerated until you need it.

> Stir together the gin, Campari, and vermouth in an ice-filled glass tumbler.

> Garnish with an orange twist. Serve with potato chips alongside.

Mains

Flank Steak *with* Salsa Verde

Serves 4 to 6

FOR THE SALSA VERDE:

2 cups Italian parsley leaves

2 cups basil leaves

¾ cup extra-virgin olive oil

½ cup capers

2 teaspoons red wine vinegar

1 teaspoon red pepper flakes

½ teaspoon kosher salt

....

1½ to 2 pounds flank steak

Kosher salt and freshly ground black pepper

Extra-virgin olive oil

O N MY LAZIEST NIGHTS, the ones when I haven't thought about dinner in advance, I'll often make flank steak. I generously season it with salt and black pepper, then cook it over a bed of hot coals or on the stovetop in a hot cast-iron pan. It's a reliable staple, especially served with salsa verde slathered all over it and an ear of boiled corn or some roasted potatoes (or try the smash-fried potatoes that accompany the Summery Sausage Bake, page 103).

But that's just one way to eat it. The cooked meat would be righteous in a steak sandwich or sliced thin and shingled over a salad; it's good in a bowl of noodle soup or subbed for the pork meatballs in the vermicelli dish on page 143. Cheaper and leaner than a rib eye, quick to cook, and equally good hot or at room temperature, flank steak can be dressed up or down, depending on your time, energy, and ingredients.

Salsa verde, a blitzed mixture of basil, parsley, capers, and vinegar, is a condiment to know. It's great with steak, but also with roasted chicken, potatoes, grilled halibut, or sardines, and it's a good way to use up bunches of herbs.

————

> In a food processor, or with a mortar and pestle, combine the parsley, basil, olive oil, capers, vinegar, red pepper flakes, and salt. Process until smooth. Let stand at room temperature at least 1 hour before serving. The sauce will keep, refrigerated, for up to 2 days; let come to room temperature before serving.

> Remove the steak from the refrigerator and season generously on both sides with salt and pepper. Drizzle with a little olive oil and let the meat come to room temperature.

> Prepare a gas or charcoal grill for direct, medium-high-heat grilling. (Alternatively, the steak can be cooked in a cast-iron frying pan on the stovetop over high heat.) Grill the steak, turning once, about 6 minutes per side for medium. Transfer to a cutting board and let stand 10 minutes, then thinly slice across the grain. Serve warm, with salsa verde alongside.

Harissa *and* Honey Chicken Thighs

Serves 4 to 6

1 red bell pepper, fresh or roasted and from a jar

1½ teaspoons cumin seeds (or 2 teaspoons ground cumin)

1 teaspoon coriander seeds (or 1¼ teaspoons ground coriander)

1 teaspoon caraway seeds (or 1¼ teaspoons ground caraway)

4 cloves garlic, peeled

1 to 2 tablespoons cayenne

1 tablespoon smoked sweet Spanish paprika

2 teaspoons kosher salt

¼ cup tomato paste

½ cup extra-virgin olive oil

2½ pounds boneless, skinless chicken thighs

2 tablespoons honey

THIS RECIPE IS really all about the harissa, which is smoky, sweet, and spicy and makes ordinary things, including sandwiches, eggs, slices of pizza, grilled steak or shrimp, even store-bought hummus, so much better. A big batch will keep for a while in the refrigerator. If it spoils before you've used it up, the problem is you, not the harissa.

If you've made the harissa in advance, this chicken recipe couldn't be simpler: Slather the thighs until coated, grill them until just cooked through, drizzle with honey (which balances out the smoke and spice), then return the chicken to the grill and cook until caramelized. If you haven't made the harissa in advance, it doesn't add a tremendous amount of time to the prep, and you can char the red bell pepper on the grill instead of roasting it in the oven.

―――

> FOR THE HARISSA: Over a gas flame (or under the broiler or on the grill), char the fresh red pepper on all sides until the skin is blackened. Transfer to a paper or plastic bag, loosely seal the bag, and let stand 10 minutes. Peel, stem, and seed the pepper. (If you're using a roasted red pepper from a jar, skip this step.) If you are using whole spices, in a small frying pan over medium-high heat, combine the cumin, coriander, and caraway seeds and toast until lightly browned and aromatic and a wisp of smoke rises from the pan, about 1 minute. Transfer to a mortar and pestle, add the garlic, and pound to a paste. Add to the bowl of a food processor. (If you're using ground spices, you can smash the garlic to a paste with the side of your knife, then add it and the ground spices to the food processor.) Add 1 tablespoon of the cayenne, the paprika, and the salt to the food processor. Add the peeled red pepper and the tomato paste and process until smooth. With the processor running, drizzle in the olive oil. Taste and season with additional cayenne. The harissa can be made ahead, then covered and refrigerated for up to 2 weeks or frozen for up to 3 months.

> In a large bowl, combine the chicken with ½ cup of the harissa (save the remaining

harissa for another use, of which there are dozens) and mix until the chicken is coated.

> Preheat a gas or charcoal grill for direct, medium-high-heat grilling. Grill the chicken, turning occasionally, until cooked through and browned on both sides, about 15 minutes. Transfer to a platter and drizzle with honey. Return the chicken pieces to the grill, and grill, turning once, until the honey caramelizes, about 2 minutes. Transfer to a platter and serve.

Spaghetti Niçoise

Serves 4

4 ounces (a good handful) green beans, stemmed

12 ounces spaghetti

¼ cup extra-virgin olive oil, plus more for finishing

3 green onions, thinly sliced

1 large clove garlic, peeled and slivered

Pinch of red pepper flakes

2 (5-ounce) cans oil-packed tuna (preferably Italian or Spanish)

2 cups halved cherry tomatoes

1 tablespoon capers

¼ cup pitted Niçoise olives

1 tablespoon white wine vinegar

½ teaspoon lemon zest

1 cup arugula

½ cup chopped Italian parsley

Kosher salt

12 large basil leaves, torn into pieces

THIS IS AN ESSENTIAL summer supper in my house, the kind of basic-with-a-twist recipe that I love. It's a riff on classic salade Niçoise, with most of the ingredients you find in that salad tossed instead with pasta, and it works spectacularly. It's light and fresh but completely satisfying, great hot or at room temperature, and manages to seem sort of special and elegant even though it's made with canned tuna.

Not all canned tuna is created equal, however, and it's worth seeking out an Italian brand of olive-oil-packed tuna, which is superior in both flavor and texture to your typical store-bought tin of fish. It's more expensive, but still less expensive than making the same dish with fresh fish; sort of a happy compromise, I think.

> Bring a large pot of salted water to a boil. When the water is boiling, add the green beans and cook until tender, 4 to 5 minutes. Remove from the pot with tongs, transfer to a colander, and rinse with cold water to stop the cooking. Cut the beans crosswise into thirds and set aside.

> Add the spaghetti to the boiling water and cook until al dente. While the pasta cooks, heat ¼ cup olive oil in a large frying pan over medium heat. Add the green onions, garlic, and red pepper flakes and cook, stirring, until the green onions soften, 1 to 2 minutes. Add the tuna (and its oil) and stir to combine, then increase the heat to medium high and add the tomatoes, capers, olives, vinegar, and lemon zest and cook, stirring, just until the tomatoes begin to soften, 2 to 3 minutes more. Remove the pan from the heat.

> Drain the spaghetti, reserving 1 cup of the pasta cooking water, and add the spaghetti to the frying pan with the tuna mixture. Using tongs, toss the pasta with the tuna mixture until well coated, adding some of the pasta cooking water as necessary. Add the green beans, arugula, and parsley and toss until combined. Season to taste with salt, then transfer to a platter and drizzle with a ribbon of olive oil. Sprinkle the basil over and serve hot or at room temperature.

Grilled Leg of Lamb with Green Onion Flatbreads

Serves 6 to 8

FOR THE LAMB:

1 tablespoon dried mint
(see note on page 88)

1 tablespoon dried oregano

1 tablespoon freshly ground
black pepper

1½ teaspoons ground ginger

1½ teaspoons ground cumin

1½ teaspoons ground coriander

1½ teaspoons ground cinnamon

1½ teaspoons ground nutmeg

½ teaspoon ground allspice

½ teaspoon ground cloves

1 (3- to 4-pound) boneless
leg of lamb

Kosher salt

3 tablespoons extra-virgin
olive oil

HSAN GURDAL, the owner of Formaggio Kitchen in Cambridge, Massachusetts (a specialty food shop and the first place I worked after college), grew up in Turkey. He introduced me, and probably many other American cooks, to baharat, a Turkish spice blend that's typically used as a seasoning for lamb. The blend varies depending on its maker, but it usually contains many of the spices Americans think of as "holiday baking spices," including cinnamon, nutmeg, allspice, and cloves, as well as dried mint. You can find premade versions at well-stocked specialty stores (including Formaggio), but it's simple to make your own.

I like to serve the lamb with grilled green onion flatbreads, which are similar to the scallion pancakes served at your local Chinese restaurant except these are grilled instead of fried. I use the pliable, chewy flatbreads as wrappers for slices of the grilled lamb. If you have any harissa (page 82) lying around, it's a killer condiment for the lamb; a cucumber-yogurt salad (chopped or grated cukes, Greek-style yogurt, lemon juice, minced garlic, and salt and pepper) would also be a nice accompaniment. Note that the lamb needs to marinate overnight or for up to two days; the flatbread dough can also be made the night before and refrigerated, but the flatbreads are best eaten hot off the grill.

FOR THE GREEN ONION
FLATBREADS:

4 cups flour

2 cups hot water

Extra-virgin olive oil,
for brushing

Kosher salt

3 cups sliced green onion tops

1½ cups chopped cilantro leaves

Melted unsalted butter,
for brushing

> In a small bowl, mix together the dried mint, oregano, black pepper, ginger, cumin, coriander, cinnamon, nutmeg, allspice, and cloves.

> Put the lamb on a work surface fat-side down. Holding a sharp knife parallel to the cutting board, slice into the thicker sections of the meat, cutting in the direction that will allow you to open the section like a book but not cutting all the way through—the goal is to butterfly the

piece of lamb to a uniform thickness so it will grill more evenly. Trim off any visible sinew or large pockets of fat. Flip the lamb over, fat-side up, and trim off and discard any excess fat cap (do not trim off all the fat, as it will baste the meat as it cooks).

> Season the lamb generously on both sides with salt, then season with the spice mixture, using all of it. Transfer to a rimmed plate or baking dish and drizzle on both sides with oil. Cover with plastic wrap and refrigerate overnight or for up to 2 days.

> Remove the lamb from the refrigerator an hour or two before you plan to grill and let come to room temperature.

> MAKE THE GREEN ONION FLATBREADS: Put the flour in a food processor. With the machine running, drizzle in the water and process until the mixture forms a ball. Transfer the dough to a lightly floured work surface and knead gently into a smooth ball. Transfer to an oiled bowl and cover with plastic wrap; let stand 30 minutes at room temperature (the dough can also be refrigerated overnight).

> Divide the dough in half. Keep one half covered with plastic wrap while you work with the other. Lightly flour a work surface and divide the half-ball of dough into 4 equal pieces. Working with one piece of dough at a time, roll the dough into an 8-inch round with a lightly floured rolling pin. Use a pastry brush to brush the dough with olive oil, then sprinkle with salt. Roll the dough away from you into a tight cylinder, then twist the cylinder into a tight spiral, tucking the end under.

> Roll the spiral into an 8-inch circle, brush with more olive oil, sprinkle with more salt, and top with some of the green onions and cilantro. Roll away from you into a tight cylinder, then twist the cylinder into a spiral, tucking the end under. Roll into an 8-inch round, then brush with olive oil and transfer, oiled-side down, to a parchment-lined baking sheet. Brush the second side with oil. Repeat the process with the remaining dough until you have 8 pancakes, separating the layers of finished pancakes with parchment paper so they don't stick together. If you

RECIPE CONTINUES ↘

plan to cook the pancakes within an hour, they can sit at room temperature. Otherwise, cover the baking sheet with plastic wrap and transfer to the refrigerator for up to 4 hours.

> Prepare a gas or charcoal grill for direct, medium-high-heat grilling. When the grill is hot, lay the lamb on the grill grate, fat-side down. Grill, flipping occasionally, until the meat is browned and an instant-read thermometer inserted in the thickest part registers 135°F, about 30 minutes. Depending on the amount of fat on the lamb, you may want to brush or drizzle the meat with additional olive oil as it cooks; it should look glistening and juicy. If the lamb is browning too quickly or if dripping fat is causing flare-ups, move the meat to a cooler part of the grill until the coals die down (if using a gas grill, lower the heat on one section of the grill and move the lamb to the cooler zone).

> Transfer to a platter and tent with foil while you grill the flatbreads. Put as many flatbreads as will fit in a single layer directly onto the grill grates. Grill, flipping occasionally with tongs, until golden brown on both sides, about 6 minutes total. Transfer to a baking sheet or plate and brush each with butter. Repeat until all the flatbreads have been grilled.

> To serve, slice the lamb into thin slices and serve with the warm flatbreads alongside.

———

Drying mint at home · *You can make dried mint in the microwave: Set fresh leaves on a plate in a single layer and microwave in 20-second increments until they're dry and crumbly. When all the leaves have been dried, push them through a fine-mesh sieve to finely grind.*

Grilled Tahini Chicken

Serves 4

1 (3- to 4-pound) chicken, cut into 10 pieces

Kosher salt

6 cloves garlic, peeled

2 teaspoons whole cumin seeds, toasted (or 2½ teaspoons ground cumin)

2 teaspoons paprika

¼ cup tahini

¼ cup lemon juice

2 tablespoons olive oil

TAHINI IS HAVING A MOMENT in the United States. Thanks in part to the popularity of Yotam Ottolenghi's cookbooks, the sesame paste has moved beyond its best-known application, as an ingredient in hummus, and now turns up in chocolate chip cookies (where it's awesome, actually), sauces, and, as in this recipe, marinades. It gives the grilled chicken an irresistible nutty richness.

One note: You must babysit this chicken on the grill, as it can char quickly. To avoid this, stand guard, tongs in hand, and once the skin has browned, turn the chicken frequently to prevent it from sticking and burning. I like to grill over hardwood charcoal, which burns hot and clean, and I maintain a two-zone fire, with a cooler area with fewer coals beneath the grate, a sort of safety zone for the chicken in case the exterior is darkening quicker than the interior can cook. If you prefer, you can also use this marinade on boneless, skin-on chicken thighs, which will cook much more quickly.

I am forever grateful to Will Gioia for teaching me this recipe. Will and his wife, Karen, cooked in many of the best Bay Area restaurants before opening their New York–style pizza spot, Gioia, in Berkeley, California, followed a few years later by a restaurant of the same name in San Francisco. They have a knack for wringing maximum flavor out of simple combinations of ingredients, as this recipe demonstrates. The chicken is terrific hot off the grill but does not suffer at all upon sitting, making it a nice do-ahead summer dish; it'd also be a great picnic dinner.

› Season the chicken pieces on both sides with salt, transfer to a plate or small baking pan, and refrigerate for at least 1 hour (or up to overnight).

› In a mortar and pestle, pound the garlic to a paste with a pinch of salt. Add the cumin seeds and pound until ground, then transfer to a bowl and add the paprika, tahini, lemon juice, and olive oil and season to taste with salt; it will have the consistency of peanut butter. (If you're using ground cumin, smash the garlic to a paste with the side of your knife, then transfer to a

RECIPE CONTINUES ↘

bowl and add the cumin and remaining ingredients.)

> Remove the chicken from the refrigerator and slather the tahini marinade all over each piece. Cover loosely with plastic wrap and let stand until the chicken is at room temperature (no more than an hour).

> Preheat a charcoal or gas grill for direct, medium-high-heat grilling. When the grill is hot, put the chicken pieces on the grill grate, skin-side down, and cook until the skin begins to brown and you can easily lift the pieces off the grate, then continue to cook, turning frequently and moving the chicken pieces from hotter to cooler parts of the grill as needed, until cooked through, about 25 to 30 minutes. The chicken has a tendency to stick, so be vigilant about turning it frequently. If the chicken threatens to burn before it's cooked through, you can move the pieces to the cooler zone of the grill, cover the grill (leaving the cover vents open), and continue grilling until it's cooked through; use a meat thermometer or the tip of a sharp knife to check.

> Transfer to a platter and serve hot or at room temperature.

Halibut Kebabs *with* Grilled Bread

Serves 4 to 6

2 pounds halibut, boned, skinned, and cut into 3-inch-by-2-inch cubes

4 cups cubed country bread, cut into 2-inch cubes

¼ cup olive oil

1 tablespoon minced fresh rosemary

1 teaspoon kosher salt

3 ounces thinly sliced pancetta

Metal or bamboo skewers (if bamboo, soak in water to cover for 1 hour before using)

'VE GOT A COUPLE OF FRIENDS who live in Alaska, and I was lucky enough to visit that strange, beautiful place one summer around the Fourth of July, when the sun never really sets. During my time there, I made a detour to the fishing town of Homer, where I sang karaoke in a bar with some naval officers who were stationed on a ship nearby. I finally stumbled out into the low light at four in the morning, thinking it was still about nine at night. (In case you are wondering, my karaoke songs of choice are Dolly Parton hits.) While I was in Homer I also took advantage of the ubiquitous, inexpensive fresh halibut, eating as much of it as I could. Shortly after returning home, I made these kebabs for the first time.

The kebabs alternate big chunks of the meaty fish, which holds up well to grilling, with cubes of bread, which basically become toasty croutons. I wrap each piece of halibut with a thin slice of pancetta, which renders as it cooks, basting the fish and the bread and eventually becoming as crispy as bacon. Cutting the fish into large cubes ensures it won't dry out on the grill. If you have leftover salsa verde (page 80) or salsa rustica (page 42), it would be good served alongside.

> Preheat a gas or charcoal grill for direct, medium-heat grilling. In a large bowl, combine the halibut, bread cubes, olive oil, rosemary, and salt and mix gently so the fish and bread are coated in oil. Let stand 10 minutes.

> Wrap each piece of fish lengthwise with a slice of pancetta, like a belt, then thread them onto the skewers lengthwise, alternating each cube of fish with a cube of bread. Lightly oil the grill grate. Set the skewers on the grill and grill the skewers until the fish and pancetta are browned on the first side and pull away easily from the grate, about 5 minutes. Flip the skewers and continue grilling until the fish is cooked through (use the tip of a small knife to check; it should be opaque and flake easily) and the pancetta and bread cubes are browned and crisp, about 6 to 8 minutes total. Transfer to a platter and serve immediately.

Rigatoni *with* Roasted Tomatoes, Ricotta, *and* Mint

Serves 4

1 cup fresh whole-milk ricotta

⅓ cup extra-virgin olive oil

1½ pounds small tomatoes, cored and halved

3 cloves garlic, peeled and slivered

Kosher salt and freshly ground black pepper

2 sprigs fresh thyme

1 sprig fresh rosemary

12 ounces rigatoni

¼ cup fresh mint leaves, finely chopped, plus some for garnish

HAVE MADE MORE PASTA in the six years since my first son was born than I'd made in all the years before that. Parents always seem to bemoan the fact that their children are subsisting on a diet of buttered noodles, but I side with the kids: pasta with salted butter and Parmigiano is one of the world's great foods. Still, it's my motherly duty to expand my kids' palates, and this pasta is straightforward enough that my boys will eat it but also interesting enough that parents dig it too.

Slow-cooking the tomatoes in a generous amount of olive oil until they slump in the pan renders them sweet and soft, even if you're beginning with less than prime specimens, and the tomato–olive oil matrix that forms in the bottom of the roasting dish becomes the light sauce for the pasta (I use this same roasting method on page 37). Instead of stirring in the ricotta, which dilutes the tomato sauce and turns it an icky pink color, I dollop it on top so you can take a bit with each bite. You can use any short dry pasta you prefer, but my children like slipping the fat rigatoni noodles on their fingers before they eat them, so that's what I use.

> Preheat the oven to 350°F. Put the ricotta in an ovenproof bowl and set aside. Pour 1 tablespoon of the olive oil into the baking dish and arrange the tomatoes in a single layer in the dish, cut-side down. Drizzle the remaining oil over the tomatoes, sprinkle the garlic over, tucking it between the tomatoes, and season with salt and pepper. Add the thyme and rosemary sprigs. Transfer to the oven and roast until the tomatoes are slumped and soft, about 30 minutes. Remove from the oven and, with your fingers, pluck off and discard the tomato skins. Transfer the tomatoes and accumulated juices to a large bowl. Turn the oven off and put the ricotta in the oven to warm slightly while you cook the pasta.

> Bring a large pot of salted water to a boil. When the water is boiling, add the pasta and cook until al dente. Drain, reserving 1 cup of the pasta cooking water, and immediately add the pasta to the bowl with the tomatoes. Stir to combine, adding some of the pasta cooking water

as needed, until the rigatoni is well coated. Add the mint and stir to mix, then transfer to a serving platter. Remove the ricotta from the oven and dollop spoonfuls of it on top of the pasta. Drizzle with a ribbon of olive oil, season with salt and pepper, and garnish with mint. Serve.

New Eggplant Parm

Serves 4 to 6

FOR THE EGGPLANT:

2½ pounds eggplant, preferably a mixture of skinny Italian and round Globe

Kosher salt and freshly ground black pepper

½ cup all-purpose flour

2 eggs, beaten

2 cups panko bread crumbs

¾ cup grated Parmigiano-Reggiano

Canola oil, for frying

FOR THE SAUCE:

2 tablespoons extra-virgin olive oil

1 cup finely chopped yellow onion (about 1 small onion)

2 cloves garlic, peeled and thinly sliced

2 pints cherry tomatoes

1 tablespoon chopped fresh oregano

Kosher salt

½ pound fresh mozzarella, torn into irregular pieces

Flaky salt, such as Maldon, for garnish

Torn basil leaves, for garnish

———

FRIED EGGPLANT is one of my favorite foods, and so I've always been drawn to eggplant Parm. But I could never understand why you'd go through all the trouble of coating slices of eggplant in bread crumbs and frying them until crispy if you were then going to freight the slices with marinara and mozzarella, causing them to go all soggy.

I understand some people don't mind this sogginess, to which I can only say, To each their own. But in my version I keep eggplant and sauce separate. I bread and fry slices of eggplant (using the same breading ingredients and technique as the Panko-Parmigiano Chicken Cutlets, page 107), then top them with mozzarella and broil just until the cheese melts. The fresh cherry tomato sauce—six ingredients, ten minutes—is served on the side so you can add as much or as little as you want.

In summertime there are usually a few different types of eggplants available at the market. I like to buy a mixture of skinny and fat ones so there is some variation in the size and texture of the fried coins.

> Cut the eggplant into ½-inch-thick slices and season the slices on both sides with salt and pepper. Put the flour in a cake pan or other rimmed dish. Put the beaten eggs in a separate cake pan or rimmed dish. In a third cake pan or rimmed dish, combine the bread crumbs and Parmigiano.

> To avoid breading your fingers, maintain one dry hand and one wet hand. Using your dry hand, dip an eggplant slice in the flour and turn to coat, then transfer the slice to the beaten eggs. With your wet hand, turn the slice to coat, then transfer it to the panko mixture. With your dry hand, turn the slice to coat on both sides, pressing lightly so the crumbs adhere. Transfer to a rimmed baking sheet and repeat with the remaining eggplant slices.

> Heat ½ inch of oil in a large heavy-bottomed frying pan

RECIPE CONTINUES ↘

over medium heat. Set a wire rack over a rimmed baking pan. When the oil is hot, add some of the eggplant slices in a single layer. Fry the eggplant, turning once, until golden brown on both sides and tender inside, about 5 to 6 minutes total. Carefully monitor the heat; if the eggplant is browning quicker than it's softening or if the bits of breading that fall into the oil are blackening, reduce the heat. Transfer the fried eggplant to the wire rack. Repeat until all the eggplant has been fried, skimming out crumbs with a slotted spoon and adding more oil to the pan as necessary.

> **MAKE THE SAUCE**: In a medium saucepan over medium heat, heat the olive oil. Add the onion and cook, stirring, until softened and translucent, about 6 minutes. Add the garlic and cook, stirring, for 1 minute more, then add the cherry tomatoes and cook, stirring, until they begin to soften and pop, about 5 minutes more. Reduce the heat to low, add the oregano, and continue cooking until the sauce thickens slightly, 5 minutes more. Season to taste with salt. Remove from the heat and transfer to a serving bowl.

> Preheat the broiler to high. Transfer the eggplant slices to an oven-safe platter, baking dish, or rimmed baking sheet, shingling the slices slightly. Top with the mozzarella and broil just until the mozzarella melts, about 2 minutes. Remove from the oven, sprinkle with flaky salt, garnish with torn basil leaves, and serve immediately, with the sauce alongside.

Summery Sausage Bake

Serves 4 to 6

1½ pounds small new potatoes (each about the size of a golf ball)

3 ears corn, shucked

¼ cup extra-virgin olive oil

Kosher salt and freshly ground black pepper

6 Italian-style pork sausages (a mix of sweet and hot)

2 cloves garlic, peeled and slivered

1 tomato, cored and quartered

1 pint cherry tomatoes

3 sprigs fresh oregano

Aioli (page 35), for serving (optional, but very good)

HAVE ALWAYS LIKED the idea of clambakes; cooking food in a pit on the beach just seems like a fun thing to do. But now, so deep into this cookbook, I think of you as a friend, so I'll just be honest: they're just never as good as I want them to be, and it's often the seafood that's the weakest link (I've been to more than one clambake where I was served semi-raw lobster).

But the supporting actors in a clambake, namely potatoes, corn, and sausage, are some of my favorite foods, so I combined them in this skillet dinner, adding in some jammy tomatoes to complete the summer supper. The technique I use on the potatoes here—boiling them whole until tender, crushing them slightly, and panfrying them until crisp—is one of my favorite ways to prepare small potatoes. Even if you never make this recipe (I don't know why you wouldn't, but that's your business), please make the spuds—they can be served as a side dish with plenty of things, like the Garlic-Butter Roast Chicken (page 115) or the Flank Steak with Salsa Verde (page 80).

Piling everything together in one big pan feels festive and generous, not unlike the clambakes that inspired it; if you don't have a frying pan large enough to accommodate everything, you can always build the bake in a deep casserole dish, a Dutch oven, or in two smaller oven-safe frying pans.

> Bring a large pot of salted water to a boil and preheat the oven to 400°F. Add the potatoes and corn to the water; cook the corn for 10 minutes, then remove with tongs and set aside. Cook the potatoes until tender but not falling apart, 5 to 10 minutes more. Drain. When the corn and potatoes are cool enough to handle, cut the corn into 1½-inch-thick wagon wheels and use the bottom of a juice glass to smash the potatoes slightly (don't press so firmly that the potatoes fall apart, just enough to crush them a bit). Transfer the smashed potatoes to a plate, drizzle with a tablespoon of olive oil, and season with salt and pepper.

> In a 12-inch heavy ovenproof frying pan (a cast-iron one is great) over medium-high heat, heat 1 tablespoon of the oil. When the oil is hot, add the potatoes and fry, turning once, until

RECIPE CONTINUES ⌄

golden brown on both sides, about 5 to 6 minutes total. Return the fried potatoes to the plate.

> Reduce the heat to medium and add the sausages to the pan (if the pan looks dry, add another tablespoon olive oil). Fry the sausages, turning occasionally, until golden brown all over but still raw within, about 5 minutes. Add the sausages to the plate with the potatoes.

> Add the garlic and the quartered tomato to the pan and cook, stirring, until the tomato begins to break down, 2 to 3 minutes. Remove the pan from the heat and add the smashed potatoes to the pan in a single layer. Add the cherry tomatoes, tucking them in around the potatoes. Lay the sausages on top of the potatoes and surround with the corn wagon wheels. Tuck in the sprigs of oregano. Season everything with salt and pepper and drizzle with another tablespoon of olive

oil. Transfer to the oven and bake until the cherry tomatoes have popped and the sausages are cooked through, about 15 minutes.

> Remove the sausages from the pan and slice crosswise into thirds. If serving in the skillet, return the sausage pieces to the skillet. Otherwise, transfer the contents of the pan to a large platter and top with the sausage. Serve with aioli alongside, if using.

Panko-Parmigiano Chicken Cutlets

Serves 4 to 6

2 pounds boneless, skinless chicken breasts

Kosher salt and freshly ground black pepper

½ cup all-purpose flour

3 large eggs, beaten

1½ cups panko bread crumbs

½ cup finely grated Parmigiano-Reggiano

Canola oil, for frying

Flaky sea salt, such as Maldon, for finishing

Lemon wedges, for serving

CHICKEN BREASTS ARE BORING, or so say all the serious food people. Never buy chicken breasts! Never, that is, unless you like crunchy, bronzed cutlets, in which case you should make these. The cutlets are endlessly versatile; I like to serve them with an arugula and fennel salad, with shaved strips of Parmigiano and a lemony vinaigrette, or on a sandwich, topped with a tangle of creamy coleslaw spiked with thin slices of jalapeño. You could also use them as the base of a killer chicken Parm—just layer the cutlets with marinara and mozzarella and bake until the cheese melts (or use the New Eggplant Parm approach on page 100 and serve the sauce alongside).

The chicken cutlets can be breaded and then frozen, uncooked, so a solid weeknight meal is always within reach. Freeze them on a wax-paper- or parchment-lined baking sheet; once frozen, transfer them to a freezer storage bag, where they'll keep for a few months. They can be fried directly from the freezer, though they'll take a few minutes longer to cook.

> Preheat the oven to 250°F. Place one hand on the top of the chicken breast. With a sharp knife, cut it in half horizontally, cutting almost but not completely through to the other side, and open like a book.

> Put the meat between two sheets of plastic wrap. Working from the center out, pound with the smooth side of a mallet or a rolling pin until the meat is ¼ inch thick. Season each piece on both sides with salt and pepper.

> Put the flour in a cake pan or other rimmed dish. Put the beaten eggs in a separate cake pan or rimmed dish. In a third cake pan or rimmed dish, combine the bread crumbs and Parmigiano.

> To avoid breading your fingers, maintain one dry hand and one wet hand. Using your dry hand, dip a cutlet in the flour and turn to coat, then transfer it to the beaten eggs. With your wet hand, turn the cutlet to coat, then transfer it to the panko mixture. With your dry hand, turn the cutlet to coat both sides, pressing lightly so the crumbs adhere. Transfer to a rimmed baking sheet and

RECIPE CONTINUES ↘

repeat with the remaining chicken.

> Heat ½ inch of oil in a large heavy-bottomed frying pan over medium heat. Set a wire cooling rack over a rimmed baking sheet. When the oil is hot, add as many pieces of the chicken as will fit in the pan in a single layer. Fry the chicken until golden brown, about 4 minutes, then flip and cook until golden brown on the second side, 3 minutes more. Transfer the chicken to the wire cooling rack set over the rimmed baking sheet and put it in the oven to keep warm. Repeat with the remaining chicken, adding more oil to the pan as necessary.

> When all the chicken has been fried, transfer it to a platter and sprinkle with flaky salt. Serve hot, with lemon wedges alongside.

Pork Saltimbocca

Serves 4 to 6

1½ pounds boneless pork loin

Kosher salt and freshly ground black pepper

12 slices prosciutto di Parma

12 whole sage leaves

2 tablespoons olive oil

2 tablespoons unsalted butter

½ cup Marsala or dry white wine

WE HAVE THE ITALIANS TO THANK for this ingenious and simple recipe that comes together in about a half an hour and can be inhaled by four hungry people in about two minutes, living up to its name, which translates to "jump in the mouth."

Sage and prosciutto are a brilliant combination (you'll see them together again in the Brown-Butter Gnocchi on page 148), capable of making even the simplest dishes incredibly flavorful.

I find it's easier to slice thin pieces of pork from a small pork loin than to butterfly and pound boneless pork chops, though of course that will work too; you could even substitute thin chicken breasts for the pork. If you want to, you can prepare the pork up to a day in advance. Then all that stands between you and dinner is a quick panfry. You could serve the saltimbocca with creamy polenta (page 124) or with a big salad, like the chicory number on page 45.

> Put the pork on a plate and transfer to the freezer. Freeze for 15 minutes. Remove from the freezer, transfer to a cutting board, and, with a sharp knife, cut into 12 thin slices. Arrange half of the slices in a single layer on a cutting board and cover with a sheet of plastic wrap. With the flat side of a meat mallet (or with a rolling pin), pound each piece of pork to a thickness of ¼ inch. Season each piece of pork on both sides with salt and pepper and transfer to a plate; repeat with the remaining slices of pork.

> Lay a slice of prosciutto lengthwise on your work surface and put one slice of pounded pork in the center. Wrap the prosciutto around the pork like a belt and

RECIPE CONTINUES ⬎

top with a sage leaf. Use a toothpick to secure the sage and prosciutto to the pork. Repeat with the remaining pork, prosciutto, and sage.

> Heat a large frying pan over medium-high heat and add the oil and butter. When the butter stops foaming, add as many slices of pork to the pan, sage-side down, as will comfortably fit in a single layer. Fry, turning once, until golden brown on both sides, about 5 minutes. Transfer to a platter, remove the toothpicks from each piece, and keep warm while you fry the remaining pork.

> When the last batch of pork has been cooked, pour the Marsala into the now-empty pan and use a wooden spoon to scrape up the browned bits from the bottom. Let boil until reduced by half, then pour over the pork. Remove the toothpicks. Serve immediately.

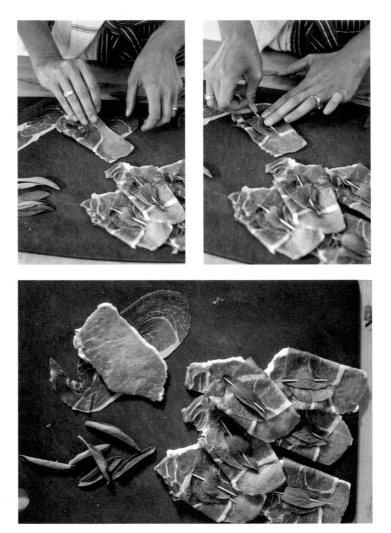

Tortilla Soup

Serves 6

1 (4-pound) whole chicken

2 large onions, peeled, 1 cut into large chunks, 1 halved and thinly sliced

2 sprigs parsley

2 sprigs fresh thyme

Kosher salt

3 tablespoons olive oil

3 cloves garlic, peeled

1 (15-ounce) can diced tomatoes

1 (20-ounce) can hominy, drained and rinsed

Canola oil, for frying

4 (6-inch) corn tortillas, sliced into ¼-inch strips

2 dried ancho chilies

Avocados, cubed, for serving

Queso fresco, cubed, for serving

Chopped cilantro, for serving

Shredded green cabbage, for serving

Lime wedges, for serving

MADE A FAIR NUMBER of proclamations about parenthood before I had children, statements that now, after having two of my own, I've, ahem, revisited. But one thing I promised myself was that I'd never make them a separate kids' dinner, believing that the kid-friendliness of a meal is in the eye of the beholder.

This is not to say that my children are world-class eaters—they are often just as deranged and choosy as most small kids—but I haven't allowed them to dictate the terms of dinner or force me to enter a tyrannical mac-and-cheese death spiral.

But I never want dinnertime to be a battlefield, so I like dinners that allow each member of my family to customize the meal. This soup is an example of one of those dinners (the vermicelli with pork meatballs, page 143, is another). I serve everyone a bowl of the mellow broth, chicken, and hominy, and then we each choose our toppings. My wife and I load ours with avocado and fried chile strips, shredded cabbage, and big squeezes of lime juice. My kids often eat theirs unadorned or make a "salad" of the tortilla strips topped with cheese cubes to eat alongside.

Adults and children alike are given the powerful feeling of control, and we sit and slurp our soup in peace (ha).

I've given instructions here on how to cut up a whole chicken and poach it quickly, yielding all the meat and stock you need for the recipe. If you prefer, you can skip that step and substitute three cups of shredded chicken (rotisserie chicken is fine) and six cups of chicken stock (yes, the low-sodium boxed kind is okay). I like to fry tortilla strips to garnish the soup, but some crumbled store-bought tortilla chips will also do the trick.

> With a sharp knife, remove the chicken wings and set aside. Cut the chicken into 2 thighs, 2 legs, and 2 breasts and remove the skin from each piece. Cut each breast crosswise into 2 pieces. With a cleaver, cut the backbone into 2-inch pieces and separate each wing in two.

Heat a Dutch oven or heavy-bottomed pot over medium-high heat and add the chicken backbone and wing pieces (and the neck, if you have it) and the large onion chunks. Cook, stirring, until the chicken pieces begin to brown, about 4 minutes. Pour

RECIPE CONTINUES ↘

in ¼ cup of water, reduce heat to low, add the parsley and thyme sprigs, cover, and cook for 20 minutes.

> Increase the heat to medium high and add 6 cups of hot water, the chicken breasts, thighs, and drumsticks, and 1 teaspoon of salt. Reduce the heat so the liquid is simmering, then cover the pot partially and simmer until the chicken pieces are just cooked through, about 20 minutes. With a slotted spoon or tongs, remove the chicken pieces and transfer to a plate. When cool enough to handle, pull the chicken meat from the bones and shred; you should have about 4 cups of meat. Strain the chicken stock through a fine-mesh strainer and discard the bones, onions, and herbs; you should have about 6 cups of chicken stock. (Skip all these steps except the shredding if you're using rotisserie chicken and store-bought chicken stock.)

> Wipe the pot clean and place over medium heat. Add 2 tablespoons of the olive oil and, when the oil is hot, add the sliced onions, whole garlic cloves, and a generous pinch of salt and cook, stirring occasionally, until the onions are golden brown, about 15 minutes. Transfer the onions and garlic to the bowl of a food processor, add the tomatoes (and their juice), and process until pureed.

> Return the pot to medium heat and add the remaining tablespoon olive oil. Add the tomato-onion puree and cook, stirring frequently, until most of the liquid has cooked out and the mixture is thick like tomato paste and beginning to stick to the pan, about 6 minutes. Pour in 6 cups of chicken stock, bring to a boil, then reduce so the liquid is simmering. Taste and adjust for seasoning, adding more salt if necessary. Add 3 cups of shredded chicken (save the rest for another use) and the hominy to the pot and simmer for 20 minutes.

> While the soup is simmering, heat ½ inch of canola oil in a medium high-sided frying pan over medium-high heat. Set a paper-towel-lined baking sheet nearby. When the oil is hot, add half of the tortilla

strips to the oil and fry until crisp, about 1 minute. Use a spider or slotted spoon to transfer the strips to the prepared baking sheet and repeat with the remaining tortilla strips. When all of the tortilla strips have been fried, add the dried chilies to the oil and fry, turning once, until brittle, about 30 seconds (do not overfry the chilies or they will turn acrid). Transfer to the prepared baking sheet; when cool enough to handle, stem, seed, and finely chop the chilies.

> Put the avocados, queso fresco, cilantro, cabbage, and lime wedges on a large platter (or in individual bowls). Put the tortilla strips in one bowl and the crumbled chilies in another. Ladle the soup into large bowls and serve, accompanied by the toppings, and let people customize their own bowls.

Garlic-Butter Roast Chicken

Serves 4

1 (3- to 4-pound) whole chicken

Kosher salt

4 tablespoons unsalted butter

3 cloves garlic, peeled

1 teaspoon coarsely ground black pepper

2 teaspoons fresh thyme leaves

THERE ARE AN ASTONISHING number of recipes for roast chicken in the world. From here on out, make your life easier—just use this one. Removing the backbone from the chicken and flattening it (a technique called spatchcocking) gives you the broadest expanse of crispy skin and speeds up the roasting process, shortening it to about an hour.

One caveat: For best results, you should salt your chicken as far in advance as possible, ideally overnight, though if life has gotten in the way and you haven't salted it the day before, even a couple of hours is beneficial and helps to dry the skin out (dry skin equals crispy skin). I prefer roasting chickens that are on the smaller side, since they cook more evenly and faster and are usually more tender. If you're feeding a larger crowd, just roast two chickens side by side.

Even if I'm forgoing the garlic butter, this is the only way I roast chickens now. If you're a purist, just season your spatchcocked bird with salt and pepper and roast it; if you want to gussy it up, serve with harissa (page 82), salsa verde (page 80), or salsa rustica (page 42). You can also use this roasted chicken for any recipe in this book calling for shredded chicken meat, like the Tortilla Soup (page 112) or Chicken and Herbed Dumplings (page 166).

> The night before you want to serve the chicken, place the chicken on a work surface, breast-side down. With a sharp knife or a pair of poultry shears, cut down along both sides of the backbone, remove it, and discard (or save for making stock). Once the backbone has been removed, use the knife or scissors to remove the keel bone, the flexible wedge of cartilage at the tip of the breastbone that connects the chicken breast to the skeleton. Discard the keel bone. Flip the chicken over and open it like a book with the pages facing down. With the heel of your hand, press firmly on the breastbone to flatten the chicken. Tuck the wing tips underneath the chicken.

> Season the chicken generously on both sides with salt, then transfer to a rimmed baking sheet or large plate and cover loosely with plastic wrap. Refrigerate overnight.

RECIPE CONTINUES ↘

> Preheat the oven to 425°F and remove the chicken from the refrigerator. Melt the butter in a small saucepan over medium-low heat. With a mortar and pestle or the edge of a knife, crush the garlic cloves. When the butter has melted, add the black pepper and toast for 30 seconds, until fragrant. Add the garlic cloves and cook until they begin to sizzle, then remove the pan from the heat and stir in the thyme. Let stand 10 minutes.

> Arrange a wire rack over a rimmed baking sheet and put the chicken on the rack, skin-side down. Pour about a quarter of the butter mixture over the chicken and rub all over, then flip the chicken skin-side up and pour over the remaining butter. Tuck the bits of garlic under the chicken (on the rack, not the baking sheet, or they will burn) and beneath the wings and the drumsticks; anywhere that they'll be protected from direct heat.

Transfer the chicken to the oven and roast, basting once or twice while cooking, until the skin is golden brown and crisp and an instant-read thermometer inserted into the thigh joint registers 170°F, about 50 minutes to 1 hour. Remove from the oven and let rest for 10 minutes, then carve, transfer to a platter, and spoon over the buttery roasting juices from the pan.

Curry Noodles *with* Beef *and* Sweet Potatoes

Serves 4 to 6

1 tablespoon canola or coconut oil, plus more for frying

1 pound fresh Chinese egg noodles (lo mein noodles)

½ cup thinly sliced shallot (1 large)

2 cloves garlic, peeled and minced

1 tablespoon prepared red curry paste

1 teaspoon ground turmeric

½ teaspoon mild curry powder

3 cups coconut milk, with ½ cup of the thickest milk set aside

½ pound beef sirloin, cut into ½-inch cubes

1 tablespoon grated palm sugar (light brown sugar can be substituted)

1 stalk lemongrass

2 Makrut lime leaves

1 small sweet potato (about 8 ounces), peeled and cut into ½-inch cubes

3 tablespoons fish sauce

1 tablespoon fresh lime juice

Cilantro leaves, to garnish

Lime wedges, for serving

1 cup chopped pickled mustard greens, for serving (optional)

THESE ARE OUTRAGEOUSLY satisfying noodles, luxuriating in a spicy coconut-milk curry, and I could eat them every week. For a dish with a simple list of ingredients that come together quickly, it has a remarkable depth of flavor. I like to top each bowl with a handful of crunchy fried noodles; it's an extra step, but a worthwhile one (if you want to use store-bought canned chow mein noodles, I'll leave that up to you). Tangy, funky pickled mustard greens are available in packages (and often in bulk) in Asian grocery stores and provide a nice counterpoint to the rich curry.

> Heat ½ inch of oil in a heavy-bottomed frying pan over medium-high heat. Line a plate with paper towels, set nearby, and measure out 4 ounces of the fresh noodles (if you don't have a scale, just grab a big handful).

> When the oil is hot but not smoking (add a small piece of noodle; it should sizzle on contact with the oil), add about 2 ounces of the noodles and fry, turning with tongs so they cook evenly, until golden brown and crisp, about 2 minutes. Use the tongs to transfer the fried noodles to the prepared plate, then fry the remaining 2 ounces noodles. Set aside.

> In a heavy-bottomed pot over medium heat, heat 1 tablespoon of canola oil. When the oil is hot, add the shallot and cook, stirring, until translucent, about 3 minutes. Add the garlic and cook for 30 seconds more, until fragrant but not browned, then stir in the curry paste, turmeric, and curry powder and cook, stirring, 30 seconds more. Add the thick coconut milk to the pot, followed by the beef, and cook just until the beef has turned color, about 3 minutes.

> Pour in the remaining 2½ cups coconut milk and add the palm sugar. Cut the

RECIPE CONTINUES ↘

woody top off the lemongrass and discard, then cut the stalk into 3-inch lengths. With the back of a heavy knife, bash the lemongrass slightly to release its fragrance. Add the lemongrass to the pot along with the lime leaves, sweet potato cubes, and fish sauce. Bring to a simmer and simmer until the sweet potatoes are tender, about 8 minutes. Reduce the heat as low as possible and cover.

> Bring a large pot of water to a boil. When the water is boiling, add the remaining egg noodles and cook until just tender. Drain.

> Uncover the curry and stir in the lime juice. To serve, put a handful of the boiled noodles in a large soup bowl and ladle some of the curry over. Garnish with cilantro leaves and some of the fried noodles. Serve hot, accompanied by lime wedges and pickled mustard greens, if using.

Broccoli Rabe *and* Mozzarella Calzones

Makes 6 calzones

FOR THE DOUGH:

1 teaspoon active instant dry yeast

2⅓ cups all-purpose flour

1 tablespoon sugar

2 tablespoons rye flour

½ teaspoon fine sea salt

2½ tablespoons olive oil

FOR THE FILLING:

2 bunches broccoli rabe

3 tablespoons olive oil, plus more for brushing

3 cloves garlic, peeled and thinly sliced

Pinch of red pepper flakes

½ cup pitted kalamata olives, halved

½ cup walnuts, toasted and chopped

¼ cup grated Parmigiano-Reggiano

Kosher salt and freshly ground black pepper

2 cups grated whole-milk mozzarella

Semolina flour, for dusting

Flaky salt, such as Maldon

A DOZEN OR SO YEARS AGO I interviewed for the position of assistant to Jeffrey Steingarten, the food writer at *Vogue* magazine and the author of two spectacular books about food. I wanted the job very badly and the interview was one of the strangest I'd ever had, involving unpacking a giant box of samples of New Zealand lamb and attempting to jam them into an overstuffed refrigerator, then joining Steingarten for a wedge of cantaloupe that he told me he had been "dry aging."

Over the melon, he quizzed me on the food world, on chefs and restaurants and trends, and at one point, the conversation turned to dark leafy greens (given the context, this is not as odd as it sounds). Steingarten is nothing if not opinionated, and I'll never forget him saying, with authority: "Only women like dark greens."

While I'm not prepared to speak for my gender as a whole, I do love greens, especially bitter broccoli rabe, also called rapini. For these calzones, I make a simple filling of cooked broccoli rabe amped up with garlic, red pepper flakes, black olives, walnuts, and Parmigiano, and I add some grated mozzarella to the half-moons before sealing them. The dough is a slight variation on the superlative pizza crust used at Chez Panisse Café and is soft and easy to work with. As with my gougères (page 51), it includes a small amount of rye flour, though it can also be made exclusively with all-purpose flour. The dough can be made ahead and frozen; thaw it completely at room temperature before rolling out and filling.

I may be insulting your intelligence by mentioning this tip, but since I just learned it myself, I figure it's worth passing along: When you're washing bowls and utensils that are coated in dough, use cold water first; it will prevent the gluten in the flour from activating and becoming that sticky web that coats your sponge.

> In a medium bowl, combine the yeast, ⅓ cup of warm water, ⅓ cup of the all-purpose flour, and the sugar. Let stand until very bubbly,

RECIPE CONTINUES ↘

30 minutes. In a large bowl, whisk together the remaining 2 cups of all-purpose flour, the rye flour, and salt. Add ½ cup of cold water and ½ cup of the flour mixture to the bowl with the yeast mixture. Mix well to combine and let sit another 30 minutes.

> Transfer the dough to the bowl of an electric mixer fitted with the dough-hook attachment and add in the remaining flour mixture and the olive oil. Knead until the dough is a soft, slightly sticky ball, about 5 minutes, adding more all-purpose flour by the tablespoonful if necessary. Transfer to a lightly oiled bowl, cover with a clean kitchen towel, and let rise in a warm, draft-free spot until doubled, about 2 hours. If you're making the dough ahead, transfer it to the refrigerator after this rise.

> Gently punch down the dough and divide into 6 pieces, each about 3½ to 4 ounces.

> Roll each piece of dough into a smooth ball, then transfer to a baking sheet. Cover lightly with plastic wrap and let stand at room temperature for an hour.

> With the dough in its final resting phase, make the filling: Bring a large pot of salted water to a boil over high heat. When the water is boiling, add the broccoli rabe and cook until just tender, about 4 minutes. With tongs, transfer to a rimmed baking sheet. When cool enough to handle, squeeze the broccoli rabe over the sink to wring out any liquid, then transfer to a cutting board and coarsely chop.

> In a large frying pan or high-sided pot, heat the olive oil over medium heat. Add the garlic and cook, stirring, for 30 seconds, until fragrant but not browned, then add the red pepper flakes and cook 10 seconds more. Add the broccoli rabe and stir to combine, then remove from the heat and let cool. Once cool, stir in the olives, walnuts, and grated Parmigiano. Season to taste with salt and pepper.

> Put a pizza stone in the oven and preheat the oven to 500°F (if you don't have a pizza stone, you can bake the calzones in a couple of large cast-iron frying pans; put the pans in the oven while it's preheating). Working with one ball of dough at a time, form the calzones. On a lightly floured work surface with a lightly floured rolling pin, roll the ball of dough into an 8-inch circle. Put some of the filling on half of the dough circle, leaving a 1-inch border. Top with ⅓ cup of the mozzarella, then bring the other half of the dough up and over the filling to form a half-moon. Fold and crimp the edges to seal, then transfer to the back of a rimmed baking sheet (or pizza peel) that has been dusted with semolina flour. Repeat with the remaining dough and filling. Brush the calzones with olive oil and sprinkle with flaky salt.

> Gently slide the calzones onto the pizza stone and bake until golden brown, about 10 minutes. Serve hot.

FOR THE RAGÙ:

3 tablespoons extra-virgin olive oil

½ cup finely diced carrots

½ cup finely diced fennel

½ cup finely diced celery

1½ pounds ground lamb

1 tablespoon tomato paste

1 cup dry red wine

1 teaspoon kosher salt

1 teaspoon fennel seeds, crushed

½ teaspoon red pepper flakes

2 cups chicken stock

1 cup canned whole tomatoes, crushed by hand

1 sprig fresh rosemary

2-inch strip orange zest (removed with a vegetable peeler)

FOR THE POLENTA:

5 cups water

1 cup polenta

2 tablespoons unsalted butter

2 tablespoons mascarpone

¼ cup grated Parmigiano-Reggiano, plus more for serving

Kosher salt

Lamb Ragù *with* Creamy Polenta

LIKE EVERY SMART PERSON in the universe, I have a real weakness for long-cooked meat sauces. They're a staple of my kitchen, and I usually have some Bolognese sauce or this lamb ragù in my freezer during the winter months, a sort of dinner insurance policy. Though the recipe takes some time, it's very simple, the action mostly unattended simmering. And though the ragù is made with ground lamb, it has a bright freshness and is warming but not heavy. If you don't have a good source for ground lamb or don't like its flavor, the ragù is equally good made with ground beef chuck. I like it spooned over creamy polenta, but it would be good with orecchiette or another similar pasta, or just on its own, with a hunk of crusty bread alongside.

> In a large high-sided pan, heat the olive oil over medium heat. Add the carrots, fennel, celery, and a pinch of salt and cook, stirring occasionally, until soft, about 8 minutes. Increase the heat to medium high, add the lamb, and cook, breaking up the chunks of meat with a wooden spoon, until the meat is no longer pink, about 5 minutes. Stir in the tomato paste and cook for 2 minutes, then pour in the wine and cook until the wine is almost completely reduced, about 5 minutes.

> Add the salt, fennel seeds, red pepper flakes, stock, tomatoes, rosemary, and orange zest and stir to combine. Bring to a boil, then reduce the heat so the liquid is gently simmering, cover partially, and cook, stirring occasionally, until the sauce has thickened and the flavors have melded, about 1½ to 2 hours. Season to taste with additional salt.

> While the ragù cooks, make the polenta: Bring the 5 cups of water to a boil in a large saucepan. Gradually add the polenta, whisking

RECIPE CONTINUES ↘

constantly as you add to prevent lumps from forming. Reduce the heat so the polenta is bubbling gently (I describe the look and sound of polenta at this stage as "La Brea Tar Pit") and cook, stirring frequently, until the polenta is tender, about 1 hour. If the polenta becomes too thick, add a bit of hot water to loosen it. Remove from the heat and stir in the butter, mascarpone, and Parmigiano and season to taste with salt. If you're not serving the polenta right away, transfer to a heatproof bowl, cover tightly with plastic wrap, and set over a saucepan of simmering water. You can hold the polenta like this for an hour, replenishing the water in the saucepan as needed.

> To serve, spoon some of the polenta into a bowl and top with a few spoonfuls of ragù. Top with grated Parmigiano and serve immediately.

Red-Chile Braised Beef

Serves 6

3½ pounds beef chuck roast, in 1 piece

Kosher salt and coarsely ground black pepper

4 dried ancho chilies (about 2 ounces), stemmed and seeded

4 dried New Mexican chilies (about 1 ounce), stemmed and seeded

4 cups chicken stock

3 tablespoons canola oil

2 white onions, peeled and thinly sliced

4 cloves garlic, peeled and thinly sliced

1 teaspoon whole cumin seeds

½ teaspoon ground coriander

1 tablespoon light brown sugar

¼ cup masa harina

THIS RICH BRAISE is a kissing cousin of chili. The braising liquid is fortified with dried chilies, then thickened just before serving with masa, which gives it a subtle, corn-y flavor. Like many braises, this one improves upon sitting; if you can make it the day before you plan to serve it, it'll be even better. The spoon-tender meat shreds easily and would make a great taco filling. Or you can serve it in larger chunks, accompanied by rice, beans (like the black beans on page 165), and tortillas or corn bread.

> Let the meat come to room temperature. Cut into 4-inch-by-3-inch chunks, trimming and discarding any large chunks of visible fat, blood vessels, or silverskin. Season the meat generously on all sides with salt and pepper.

> Put the chilies in a dry heavy-bottomed pot or high-sided frying pan over medium-high heat. Toast the chilies, turning frequently, until dry and fragrant, about 3 minutes. Pour in the chicken stock, bring to a boil, then reduce the heat so the liquid is simmering and simmer for 20 minutes. Remove from the heat and, with an immersion blender (or in a tabletop blender), blend until smooth. Set aside.

> In a large Dutch oven, heat the canola oil over high heat. When the oil is shimmering but not smoking, add the beef and sear until deeply browned on all sides, about 10 minutes (if your Dutch oven is not large enough to accommodate all the beef in a single layer, sear it in two batches, adding more oil if necessary). Transfer the beef to a rimmed plate and pour off all but 1 tablespoon of the oil. Reduce the heat to medium and add the onions and garlic and cook, stirring, until the onions begin to soften, about 5 minutes. Add the cumin and coriander and cook 30 seconds more. Pour the chile liquid into the pot and add the brown sugar. Season to taste with salt.

> Return the meat to the pot, bring to a boil, then reduce the heat so the liquid is simmering gently. Cover partially and cook, stirring occasionally, until the beef is fork-tender, about 2½ to 3 hours. The beef can

RECIPE CONTINUES ↘

be prepared up to this point, cooled to room temperature, then refrigerated for up to 3 days. Use a spoon to remove any fat that has congealed on top. Reheat gently over low heat until the meat is warmed through, then proceed with the remaining steps.

> In a small bowl, stir together the masa harina and ¼ cup water to make a thick paste. Stir the paste into the chile sauce, cover partially, and let cook 10 minutes, stirring occasionally.

> To serve, transfer the beef chunks and sauce to a serving bowl. (Alternatively, you can use two forks to shred the beef into the sauce.) Serve with rice, beans, tortillas, or corn bread alongside.

PANTRY PASTAS

Cacio e Pepe

Serves 4

12 ounces spaghetti

6 tablespoons unsalted butter

2 teaspoons coarsely cracked
black pepper

1 cup finely grated Parmigiano-
Reggiano (use a Microplane
or the smallest holes of
a box grater)

⅔ cup finely grated Pecorino
Romano (use a Microplane
or the smallest holes of
a box grater)

For a recipe that has only five ingredients, this Roman pasta dish is crazy-delicious, the kind of late-night, empty-fridge recipe that dreams are made of. And while it has few ingredients, the success of the dish relies almost totally on technique, and it may take you a few attempts to perfect it. But once you've mastered it, this recipe—made entirely with things you probably always have on hand—is yours forever.

Rather than drain the pasta through a colander when it's ready, I use tongs to transfer it directly from the water to the pan containing the butter and toasted black pepper, then I add the Parmigiano and toss. Some of the cooking water clings to the noodles and the pot is at my elbow if I need to add a bit more of that starchy water to help the butter sauce emulsify. The amount of pasta water to add depends on the brand of dried pasta you're using; it gets easier to figure out with experience. You want to add enough to aid the melting of the hard cheese but not so much that the sauce becomes watery; the goal is a bowl of al dente noodles cloaked in a creamy sauce made from the combination of butter, cheese (I use a mixture of Parmigiano-Reggiano and Pecorino Romano), and that starchy pasta cooking water.

I like the Rustichella d'Abruzzo brand of dried pasta. If you can't find it, look for another Italian brand that is extruded through bronze dies (the label will likely boast of this), which gives the exterior of each noodle a rougher texture, something the sauce can cling to.

> Bring a large pot of salted water to a boil; add the pasta and cook until al dente.

> Meanwhile, melt the butter in a heavy frying pan over medium heat. Add the pepper and cook, swirling the pan, until it begins to sizzle, about 1 minute. Set aside.

> When the pasta is al dente, use tongs to transfer it to the frying pan and place the pan over low heat (keep the pot of pasta water nearby:

you may need it). Add the Parmigiano and ½ cup of the pasta cooking water to the frying pan and, with tongs, immediately toss the pasta until the cheese melts; you want to keep everything moving so the cheese doesn't sink to the bottom of the pan and start clumping. If a film of cheese begins to form on the bottom of your pan, reduce the heat and continue tossing. Add more pasta cooking water as necessary; the sauce should be creamy and emulsified and coat each strand of pasta.

> Remove from the heat, stir in the Pecorino, and toss to coat. Transfer to bowls and serve hot.

Bucatini all'Amatriciana

Serves 4 to 6

MY WIFE AND I went to Italy with our older son when he was just about a year old. We spent a week in Rome, and I have many happy memories of that period, including watching our son, a bowlegged new walker, toddle around the piazzas in a tiny pair of all-American Wrangler's, chasing after pigeons. We fell into an easy routine in Italy, one that included daily doses of gelato and pasta. I always ordered the cacio e pepe and my wife got the bucatini all'Amatriciana, and we'd pass the bowls back and forth between us, fishing out noodles for the baby to try.

Though you can substitute spaghetti for the traditional fat, hollow bucatini noodles, I recommend using bucatini if you can find it. And because this recipe has only a handful of ingredients, use good ones—best-quality canned tomatoes (I like the Bianco DiNapoli brand), good quality pancetta, and real Pecorino Romano.

If the version I make at home doesn't taste quite like the pasta we ate in Roman trattorias, I blame the environment, not the recipe.

2 tablespoons olive oil

8 ounces pancetta, diced into ½-inch pieces

½ small red onion, peeled and finely diced

1 (28-ounce) can whole tomatoes, crushed by hand, juice reserved

1 teaspoon red pepper flakes

Kosher salt and pepper

1 pound bucatini or spaghetti

½ cup grated Pecorino Romano, plus more for serving

> Heat the oil in a large high-sided frying pan over medium-low heat. Add the pancetta and cook, stirring frequently, until it is browned and has rendered its fat, about 15 minutes. Remove from the pan with a slotted spoon and reserve.

> Add the red onion to the pan, increase the heat to medium, and cook, stirring occasionally, until the onion is translucent, about 5 minutes.

Pour in the tomatoes and their juice, add the red pepper flakes, and season to taste with salt and pepper. Reduce the heat and simmer the sauce for 25 minutes, stirring occasionally. Taste and adjust seasoning. Stir in the reserved pancetta.

> Bring a large pot of salted water to a boil. Add the bucatini and cook until al dente. Drain the pasta, reserving a cup of the pasta cooking water. Add the pasta and grated Pecorino to the frying pan containing the sauce and toss to coat, adding some of the reserved pasta water as necessary; the sauce should coat the noodles and be glossy, but don't add so much water that it becomes watery.

> Transfer to warmed plates and serve with additional Pecorino alongside.

Aglio e Olio

Serves 4

⅔ cup plus 2 tablespoons
extra-virgin olive oil

1 cup fresh bread crumbs

Kosher salt

6 cloves garlic, peeled and
sliced paper-thin

¼ teaspoon red pepper flakes

12 ounces spaghetti

½ cup parsley leaves

Freshly ground black pepper

SPEND MOST OF MY DAYS working from home, my laptop set up on our kitchen table, and when lunchtime rolls around, I usually do a leftovers dive in the refrigerator. But on the days that I'm willing to put in a bit more effort, this is what I'll make for myself. I always have these ingredients on hand, and strands of oil-slicked spaghetti punctuated by paper-thin slivers of garlic, red pepper flakes, and parsley are both quick to make and comforting to eat.

Note: This spaghetti is also very good late at night if you've maybe had a bit too much to drink and you want a little ballast in your stomach before you head to bed. You could even top it with a fried egg.

———

> Heat a large frying pan over medium heat and add 2 tablespoons of the olive oil. Add the bread crumbs and stir to coat with oil. Toast the bread crumbs, stirring, until dark golden brown and very crunchy, about 5 to 6 minutes. Transfer to a paper-towel-lined plate and season with salt. Set aside.

> Bring a large pot of salted water to a boil over high heat. In the same large frying pan, combine the remaining ⅔ cup olive oil, garlic, and red pepper flakes. Cook, stirring, until the garlic begins to sizzle and turns a very pale golden color (do not let it brown, or it will become acrid). Remove from the heat.

> Add the pasta to the boiling water and cook until al dente. Drain, reserving 1 cup of the pasta cooking water. Return the frying pan with the oil-and-garlic mixture to medium heat and add ¼ cup of the pasta cooking water. Bring to a boil, swirling the pan so the water and oil emulsify. Add the spaghetti and use tongs to toss the pasta with the oil and garlic so each strand of spaghetti is coated, adding more pasta cooking water if necessary. Add the parsley and bread crumbs and toss to mix, then season with black pepper and additional salt and serve.

Hot-Dog Fried Rice

Serves 4

4 cups cooked, cooled white rice

Kosher salt

Sugar

1 cup (about 4 ounces) small broccoli florets

2 medium carrots

¼ cup canola oil

4 green onions, thinly sliced

2 hot dogs, diced

2 eggs, beaten with a pinch of salt

1½ tablespoons Golden Mountain Seasoning Sauce

1 tablespoon soy sauce

½ cup frozen peas, thawed

1 cup spinach leaves or thinly sliced Swiss chard leaves

⅓ cup chopped cabbage kimchi (optional)

FRIED RICE is part of my culinary dowry, something my mother made often and well, using whatever scraps were left in the refrigerator. I've tested this with many ingredients, stirring in cubed ham, leftover shredded pork, rotisserie chicken, grilled shrimp, and a panoply of vegetables ranging from broccoli and spinach to zucchini and fennel. Somehow, it always works; fried rice is the great equalizer.

The eggs and green onions are nonnegotiable, however, and that duo, along with soy sauce, is what I think really gives fried rice its signature flavor. An unabashed lover of hot dogs, with the freezer stock to prove it, I like to dice a couple and add them in. Of course, you could omit them for a completely satisfying vegetarian dish, or use other bits of leftover meat, like roast pork, steak, or roasted chicken.

The best fried rice is made with day-old white rice. Its slight dryness prevents it from becoming mushy as it's tossed in the pan. If you don't have leftover rice, cook some at least a few hours in advance of frying. Once the rice is cooked, turn it out onto a rimmed baking sheet and spread it in a thin layer, which will help it cool more quickly and dry it out a bit. In a real pinch, I've also purchased cooked rice from my local takeout spot (yes, I could just buy fried rice there instead, but I don't—which says something about how highly I regard my homemade version).

Golden Mountain Seasoning Sauce is a Thai condiment made from fermented soybeans, salt, and sugar. If you can't find it, substitute additional soy sauce, salt, and sugar to taste. If you'd like, you can stir in some chopped cabbage kimchi at the end.

Have your ingredients prepped and nearby before you start making fried rice. Start to finish, the cooking will take under ten minutes.

> Season the rice with a generous pinch of salt and sugar. Steam the broccoli and carrots just until tender; cut the broccoli florets into very small pieces and dice the carrots.

> In a large frying pan over high heat, heat the oil. When the oil is hot, stir in the green onions and hot dogs and cook, stirring, until the green onions sizzle and soften and

RECIPE CONTINUES ↘

the pieces of hot dog begin to brown, about 2 minutes. Pour in the beaten eggs and cook, stirring with a rubber spatula, until they begin to scramble. Stir in the rice and add the seasoning sauce and soy sauce and mix to combine, then cook, stirring, for 2 minutes. Stir in the broccoli, carrots, and peas and stir to combine. Stir in the spinach and kimchi, if using, and cook, stirring, until the spinach wilts and the kimchi is heated through, 2 to 3 minutes more. Season to taste with additional salt, seasoning sauce, or soy sauce.

Beef Albóndigas

Makes 16 meatballs

2 tablespoons white rice, uncooked

5 eggs

1½ pounds ground beef

½ small white onion, peeled and finely chopped (about ½ cup)

2 cloves garlic, peeled and minced

3 tablespoons finely chopped cilantro

2 tablespoons finely chopped mint

1 tablespoon olive oil

2 teaspoons kosher salt

2 cups tomato sauce (canned or homemade, page 145)

1 cup chicken stock

1 tablespoon minced canned chipotle chilies in adobo sauce plus 2 teaspoons adobo sauce from the can

2 cinnamon sticks

1 bunch spinach (preferably not baby spinach), stemmed and washed (about 4 cups)

Steamed rice, for serving

CAN COUNT ON THE FINGERS of one hand the number of times my father cooked dinner for me and my siblings when we were kids. On the rare occasions that my mother was out of town or too ill to leave bed, my father would turn to the bachelor's stalwart companion—a pound of ground chuck, its possibilities limitless. On one such evening, he made meat loaf, dutifully following a recipe he'd tracked down somewhere. My brother, sister, and I took our seats at table as he sliced the loaf, and we all registered horror the moment we saw that the interior of the meat loaf was studded with hard-cooked eggs.

So it's with no small amount of irony that I share these meatballs, a recipe adapted from one a reader submitted to *Sunset* magazine when I was working there as an editorial assistant. The ground beef is seasoned with garlic, cilantro and mint, and formed around a chunk of hard-cooked egg. (If hard-cooked eggs aren't your thing, substitute cubes of queso fresco or omit the stuffing altogether.) The meatballs are simmered in a chipotle-spiked tomato sauce, and because they aren't browned first, some of the meat sloughs off into the sauce and enriches it (I use this same poaching method for the meatballs in tomato sauce, page 145). The addition of spinach to the sauce makes this a one-dish meal; serve it with rice to absorb the sauce.

> Put the uncooked rice in a small bowl and add cold water to cover. Let soak 20 minutes, then drain. Put 4 of the eggs in a medium saucepan and add cold water to cover. Bring to a boil over high heat, boil for 1 minute, then remove from the heat and cover. Let stand 8 minutes, then transfer the eggs to an ice-water bath. When cool, carefully peel the eggs and quarter them. Set aside.

> In a large bowl, add the drained rice, beef, onion, garlic, cilantro, mint, olive oil, salt, and the remaining (raw) egg and mix well to combine. Take a small amount of the meat mixture and use your hands to form it into a thin patty. Place a hard-boiled egg quarter in the center of the patty, then fold the meat mixture around the egg,

RECIPE CONTINUES ⬎

enclosing it completely, and shape into a sphere. Repeat with the remaining meat and eggs until you've made 16 meatballs.

> Pour the tomato sauce and chicken stock into a large high-sided saucepan or pot. Add the minced chipotles, adobo sauce, and cinnamon sticks and stir to combine. Put the meatballs in the pot, arranging them snugly in a single layer (the meatballs will be poking out of the sauce). Bring to a boil over medium-high heat, then reduce the heat so the sauce is simmering gently. Cover and cook for 10 minutes, stirring gently after the meatballs have cooked for 5 minutes.

> Use a slotted spoon to transfer the meatballs to a serving dish. Remove the cinnamon sticks from the sauce and discard, then increase the heat so the sauce is simmering vigorously. Stir in the spinach and cook until the spinach is wilted, about 5 minutes, then pour the sauce over the meatballs. Serve hot, accompanied by white rice.

FOR THE MEATBALLS:

2 stalks lemongrass

2 pounds ground pork

1 tablespoon fish sauce

2½ teaspoons kosher salt

2 teaspoons sugar

¼ teaspoon white pepper

FOR THE DRESSING:

¼ cup fish sauce

2 tablespoons sugar

2 tablespoons lime juice or white vinegar

1 clove garlic, peeled and minced

1 Thai chile or half of a serrano chile, stemmed and minced

FOR THE FRIED SHALLOTS:

2 cups canola oil

4 shallots, peeled and thinly sliced

....

1 pound rice vermicelli

2 carrots, peeled and julienned

1 small cucumber, peeled and thinly sliced

Shredded lettuce, for serving

Mint leaves, for serving

Cilantro leaves, for serving

Chopped peanuts, for serving

Vermicelli Noodles *with* Lemongrass Pork Meatballs

I HAD THE BEST VERSION of these noodle bowls in Hanoi on a trip my wife and I took before our children were born. At the second-story restaurant, in catbird seats overlooking the busy street, we were served a giant bowl of meatballs, a mountain of vermicelli, an enormous platter of herbs, and lots of condiments on the side. Whenever supplies dipped low, the bowls and platter would be replenished. Free refills! It was the meal of a lifetime.

These noodle bowls are great any time of year, but because the noodles are served cold, they're especially nice on a sweltering day. In that case, the pork meatballs can also be grilled; I form them into small patties, about two inches across and half an inch thick, then grill them over a medium hot grill, turning as needed, until caramelized on the outside and cooked within, about 6 to 8 minutes.

This recipe can be made ahead, scaled up for a crowd, and easily customized to any diner's taste. My children prefer theirs relatively plain, just a pile of noodles, a couple of meatballs, and a handful of peanuts.

The rest of us add spoonfuls of the sweet-spicy dressing and lots of herbs, and we fight over the last spoonful of fried shallots, which are irresistible. You might want to get in the habit of keeping them around, because they're also great on top of green salads, on macaroni and cheese or other creamy pastas, and on sandwiches of all kinds.

> MAKE THE MEATBALLS: Cut the bottom ½ inch off each lemongrass stalk and trim the woody top portion of each stalk and discard. Peel the outer layers of each stalk until you reach the tender center. Thinly slice the stalks into coins, then very finely mince. Transfer to a medium bowl and add the pork, fish

RECIPE CONTINUES ↘

sauce, salt, sugar, and white pepper and mix to combine. Roll into 1½-inch meatballs and set on a rimmed baking sheet. The meatballs can be made beforehand; transfer to a lidded container or tightly wrap the baking sheet with plastic wrap. Refrigerate until ready to use but no longer than 24 hours.

> MAKE THE DRESSING: In a small jar with a lid, combine the fish sauce, sugar, lime juice, garlic, and minced chile. Put the lid on the jar and shake vigorously until the sugar has dissolved. Set aside (the dressing will keep, refrigerated, for up to a week, though it gets spicier as it sits).

> MAKE THE FRIED SHALLOTS: Pour the oil into a medium heavy-bottomed saucepan over medium heat and add the sliced shallots to the cold oil. Line a plate with paper towels and set it nearby. As the oil heats, the shallots will begin to sizzle and bubble; fry, stirring frequently for even cooking, until the shallots begin to brown, about 6 to 8 minutes. Continue cooking, stirring

constantly, until they are an even golden brown and crisp (at this stage, they can go from nicely browned to acrid and overcooked very quickly, so be vigilant). Use a spider or slotted spoon to transfer the shallots to the paper-towel-lined plate. Let the oil cool, then pour through a fine-mesh sieve into a clean jar. (Do not discard the oil; it's liquid gold, great for another batch of fried shallots or to add flavor to dressings and sautéed vegetables, and you can also use it to make a batch of aioli.) The fried shallots can be made in advance. Let cool, then store in an airtight container at room temperature. Resist snacking on them; they'll keep for about a week.

> Bring a large pot of water to a boil. When the water is boiling add the vermicelli noodles and cook according to package instructions until tender. Drain, rinse with cold water, and transfer to a rimmed baking sheet. Drizzle with a tablespoon of the shallot oil (it's fine if it's still warm) and toss to coat.

> Preheat the broiler to high. Transfer the baking sheet of meatballs to the oven, positioning it a few inches from the heating element. Broil the meatballs until browned, about 3 minutes, then roll the meatballs to the second side and broil for 3 minutes longer. Transfer to a bowl.

> To serve, arrange the vermicelli on a platter and surround with carrots, cucumber slices, lettuce, mint, and cilantro leaves. Serve the meatballs, dressing, fried shallots, and chopped peanuts alongside. Let the diners dig in, serving themselves some of the noodles, carrots, and cucumbers, garnished with herbs, shallots, and peanuts. Spoon dressing over each serving and top with a few meatballs.

FOR THE SAUCE:

2 (28-ounce) cans whole tomatoes (I like Bianco DiNapoli brand)

¼ cup extra-virgin olive oil

5 cloves garlic, peeled and slivered

1 teaspoon red pepper flakes

Kosher salt

3 sprigs fresh basil

FOR THE MEATBALLS:

1 cup fresh bread crumbs

⅓ cup whole milk

8 ounces ground beef chuck

8 ounces ground pork

½ cup finely ground Parmigiano-Reggiano

½ cup finely chopped Italian parsley

1 teaspoon salt

½ teaspoon freshly ground black pepper

2 large eggs

2 cloves garlic, peeled and finely minced

Beef-and-Pork Meatballs *in* Tomato Sauce

SEVEN OR SO years ago, my meatball quest came to an end when I discovered that Molly Wizenberg—writer, restaurant owner, kindred spirit—had been on the same quest and had finally found a recipe that was perfect. *Oh, good!* I thought. *Thank you for doing the work for me.*

Molly might not know it, but she's partially responsible for this cookbook. She shared her meatball recipe (which she learned from the chefs at Seattle's Café Lago) in an article in *Bon Appétit,* and in the last line, she wrote, "That's the beauty of a repertoire: that in drawing from a whole world of recipes, you wind up making your own." Yes! Molly gets it.

I didn't do much to her recipe, honestly. I fiddled a bit with the amount of each ingredient, upping the parsley and decreasing the Parmigiano, but these were just little tweaks, the process of making a recipe one's own. Molly favors Marcella Hazan's butter-enriched tomato sauce, and there's nothing wrong with that, but I use my own tried-and-true recipe. We agree, however, that there's no point in cooking the meatballs before adding them to the sauce. If you poach them in the tomato sauce, they're extremely tender, and some of their meaty, cheesy goodness fortifies the sauce.

If you don't want to make your own sauce, these meatballs are equally good poached in store-bought marinara sauce, the sort of semi-homemade hack that is essential for any working parent or busy person in the world. Choose a jarred sauce with a very short ingredient list, preferably one that doesn't include sugar.

Ground Parmigiano (as opposed to grated) makes a difference here. The easiest way to do it is to pulse some cubed cheese in the food processor until it has the texture of coarse sand.

> Pour the tomatoes into a bowl and use your hands to crush them. Combine the olive oil, garlic, and red pepper

RECIPE CONTINUES ↘

flakes in a heavy-bottomed pot over medium-low heat. Cook, stirring, until the garlic turns the palest golden color (keep an eye on it; you don't want the garlic to brown). Add the tomatoes, a few teaspoons of salt, and the basil sprigs.

> Bring to a lively simmer, then reduce the heat so the sauce is bubbling gently. Cook, stirring occasionally, until the sauce has thickened and reduced and a slick of oil has risen to the top, about 1 hour. Remove from the heat, stir vigorously, and season to taste with salt. The sauce can be used immediately or cooled to room temperature, covered, and refrigerated; the cooled sauce can also be frozen in plastic storage bags for up to 3 months. (I pour the sauce into quart-size bags, lay them flat on a baking sheet, then freeze, still on the baking sheet, until solid. That way they stack neatly in the freezer.)

> While the sauce cooks, make the meatballs: Put the bread crumbs in a bowl and pour the milk over. Let stand 10 minutes, then use your hands to remove the crumbs from the bowl, squeezing to remove the excess milk. Transfer the soaked crumbs to a large bowl and discard the milk. Add the remaining ingredients and mix gently but thoroughly to combine (don't overwork the mixture or the meatballs will be tough). Form into 1½-inch meatballs, set on a rimmed baking sheet or plate, and cover with plastic wrap. Refrigerate until ready to cook; the meatballs can be made up to a day ahead.

> Add the meatballs to the finished pot of simmering tomato sauce, cover, and cook, stirring occasionally, until cooked through, about 15 minutes (cut one to test). If you're planning to serve the meatballs with spaghetti, bring a large pot of salted water to a boil and add the spaghetti to the water at the same time you add the meatballs to the sauce; this makes enough sauce for 1 pound of dry pasta.

Brown-Butter Gnocchi *with* Crispy Prosciutto *and* Sage

Serves 4

2 pounds russet potatoes (about 3 medium)

6 tablespoons unsalted butter

1 egg

¼ cup plus 2 tablespoons finely grated Parmigiano-Reggiano

1 teaspoon kosher salt

1 cup all-purpose flour

Extra-virgin olive oil

4 ounces thinly sliced prosciutto

15 sage leaves

Freshly ground pepper

WHEN I WAS A KID, I'd always ask for meat loaf and mashed potatoes as my birthday meal. And these days, when I'm sick or sad, I bake myself a potato and load it with pats of salted butter.

Gnocchi, which likely originated in northern Italy, is a pasta made from potatoes, and it's really just a sophisticated form of comfort food. I've never particularly liked the combination of gnocchi with tomato sauce; the sauce masks their delicate flavor. But gnocchi tossed in nutty brown butter with crispy bits of prosciutto and sage leaves? That makes sense.

Adding too much flour to gnocchi dough can cause them to be leaden and dense, but if you don't add enough, they'll fall apart when boiled. Practice makes perfect—you're looking for a dough that is soft but not sticky, and the amount of flour that you add to each batch may change, since the moisture content of the potatoes (and flour) can vary.

> Preheat the oven to 400°F. Rinse the potatoes and place them on a rimmed baking sheet. With a fork, poke holes in each potato. Bake until tender, about 1 hour. Remove from the oven and when just cool enough to handle but still very warm, split the potatoes in half and scoop out the flesh. Discard the skin. Pass the potato flesh through a ricer onto a rimmed baking sheet and spread in an even layer.

> Melt 2 tablespoons of the butter. In a small bowl, whisk together the melted butter, egg, 2 tablespoons of the Parmigiano, and the salt. Drizzle over the warm riced potatoes, then sprinkle about ¾ cup of the flour over. With your fingertips, gently work the mixture into a ball. The dough should be soft but not sticky; if it's sticky, add some of the remaining flour by the tablespoonful. Form the dough into a disk and cut the disk into 1-inch slices. Roll each slice into a ball.

> Lightly dust a rimmed baking sheet with flour and set nearby. On a lightly floured work surface, working with one ball of dough at a time, roll into a snake about ¾ inch around. Cut each snake crosswise into ¾-inch pieces. Using your thumb

RECIPE CONTINUES ↘

and one piece of dough at a time, roll each piece across a gnocchi paddle or the tines of an overturned fork, pressing down lightly so the gnocchi curve around your thumb slightly, then drop onto the prepared baking sheet. Repeat with the remaining balls of dough until all of the gnocchi have been formed. (You can make the gnocchi to this point, freeze them on the baking sheet, and then transfer them to plastic freezer storage bags. They can be boiled from frozen.)

> Bring a large pot of salted water to a boil. Drizzle a rimmed baking sheet with a small amount of olive oil. When the water is boiling, add the gnocchi to the water in batches. The gnocchi will sink and then float; when they rise to the top, boil them for 2 minutes. With a spider or slotted spoon, transfer the gnocchi to the baking sheet.

> Heat a large nonstick frying pan over medium heat. Lay a few slices of the prosciutto in the pan in a single layer and cook, turning once, until crispy, about 2 minutes. Transfer to a plate and repeat until all of the prosciutto has been fried. Add the remaining 4 tablespoons butter to the pan and, when it melts, add the sage leaves and fry until crisp. Transfer the fried sage to the plate with the prosciutto.

> Let the butter continue to cook until it's light golden brown and has a nutty aroma. Slide the gnocchi into the pan and, with a rubber spatula, stir gently to coat the gnocchi in butter. Cook without stirring until the gnocchi are heated through and beginning to develop a golden-brown crust on the bottom, about 2 minutes. Crumble the prosciutto into the pan and stir gently with the rubber spatula to combine. Season to taste with salt and pepper, then transfer to a platter and garnish with the fried sage and remaining ¼ cup grated Parmigiano. Serve immediately.

Rustic Seafood Stew

Serves 4

3 tablespoons extra-virgin olive oil, plus more for toasts

1 cup finely diced leeks (about 1 medium leek)

¾ cup finely diced fennel

4 cloves garlic, peeled (3 thinly sliced, 1 left whole)

Kosher salt and freshly ground black pepper

¾ cup dry white wine

1 bay leaf

1 sprig fresh thyme

¼ teaspoon red pepper flakes

2 cups bottled clam juice

1 cup diced fresh tomatoes or 1 (15-ounce) can diced tomatoes, drained

½ pound fingerling potatoes, sliced into ¼-inch coins

1 baguette, cut diagonally into long, thin slices

½ pound Manila or littleneck clams, scrubbed

½ pound mussels, scrubbed and debearded

½ cup finely chopped parsley

10 large shrimp, peeled and deveined

½ pound squid, tubes and tentacles, tubes cut into ¼-inch-thick rings

½ pound firm white fish, such as halibut or cod, cut into 1½-inch cubes

Aioli (page 35), for serving

'VE LISTENED TO ENOUGH *Chez Panisse* gospel and lived in California long enough to know that good ingredients really do improve almost every recipe. But there are some recipes, like this one, that absolutely hinge on the quality of the ingredients. Great seafood stew is an easy recipe, one that makes the cook look good, and it can be mastered by even the greenest one out there. The secret is to buy the best fish and shellfish you can find and not overcook it. There's not much more to it.

I use a nice mixture of clams, mussels, shrimp, squid, and fish, but the beauty of a seafood stew is that it's flexible, so you can adjust the quantities and types of seafood you use depending on what's available and what you like, though I do encourage a mixture of shellfish and fish. It makes the stew feel fully loaded and luxurious, with a mix of flavors and textures. I use bottled clam juice because it's readily available; I almost never have homemade fish stock on hand. If you do, you can substitute it for the clam juice.

The stew is simple enough for a family supper but feels special enough to serve to guests. Adding a spoonful of aioli to each bowl enriches the broth with garlicky flavor.

> Preheat the oven to 350°F. Heat 3 tablespoons olive oil in a large Dutch oven or heavy pot over medium heat. Add the leeks, fennel, and sliced garlic and season with salt and pepper. Cook, stirring, until the leeks are translucent but not brown and the fennel has softened, about 6 minutes. Pour in the wine and cook, stirring occasionally, until the wine has evaporated, 3 to 4 minutes. Add the bay leaf, thyme, and red pepper flakes and pour in the clam juice.

RECIPE CONTINUES ↘

Bring to a gentle simmer and add the tomatoes and potatoes. Simmer until the potatoes are just tender, about 10 minutes.

> Arrange the baguette slices on a rimmed baking sheet and brush both sides generously with olive oil. Transfer to the oven and bake until crisp and golden, about 8 minutes. Season with salt, then rub the remaining whole clove of garlic once over the surface of each toast. Keep warm.

> Put 1 inch of water in a large saucepan or heavy pot. Bring to a boil over high heat, add the clams and mussels, cover, and steam until the shells open (discard any clams or mussels that don't open), about 5 minutes. Turn off the heat.

> Season the broth to taste with additional salt and pepper and add the parsley. Add the shrimp, squid, and fish to the broth, cover, and cook until the shrimp are bright pink and the cubes of fish are cooked through, about 5 minutes. With a slotted spoon or tongs, transfer the steamed clams and mussels to the broth, then stir gently with a spoon to combine. Divide the soup among warmed bowls, making sure each serving has some shrimp, squid, clams, mussels, and fish. Serve hot, accompanied by the toasts and aioli.

Cider-Braised Chicken *with* Fall Vegetables

Serves 4 to 6

5 small parsnips (about 10 ounces)

⅓ pound pancetta or bacon, diced

8 bone-in, skin-on chicken thighs (about 3 pounds)

Kosher salt and freshly ground black pepper

1 small yellow onion, peeled and finely diced

2 small cloves garlic, peeled

1½ cups dry hard apple cider

1 cup chicken stock

3 medium carrots, peeled and cut into ½-inch-thick batons

2 sprigs fresh thyme

2 cups Brussels sprouts, halved

UNLIKE MOST BRAISED DISHES, this stovetop chicken braise cooks quickly, making it a good choice for a weeknight meal. Because of the cozy connotations of braising (and the parsnips and Brussels sprouts), it's a recipe I usually make in the colder months using yeasty hard apple cider as the braising liquid. There are many brands of hard cider available now, but I suggest looking for a dry cider, preferably a farmhouse one that has some yeasty, barnyard funk; the parsnips and carrots add enough sweetness. If you can't find dry hard cider, you could substitute a fifty-fifty blend of apple cider and dry white wine.

Adding the Brussels sprouts at the end of the braising time prevents them from turning into mushy, drab orbs. I like to serve this braise with buttered tagliatelle or egg noodles, but mashed potatoes would also be good; you want something to soak up the thin, flavorful braising liquid.

―――

> Preheat the oven to 325°F. Peel the parsnips and cut into ½-inch-thick batons. With the tip of a paring knife, pry out and discard the woody core from each parsnip baton. Set aside. In a Dutch oven over medium heat, add the pancetta. Cook the pancetta, stirring, until the fat has rendered and the pancetta is browned, about 6 minutes. Remove the pancetta with a slotted spoon and transfer to a paper-towel-lined plate.

> Pat the chicken dry with paper towels and season on both sides with salt and pepper. Increase the heat in the Dutch oven to medium high and put the chicken in the pan, skin-side down; cook in batches if necessary. Cook until golden brown, about 6 minutes, then flip the chicken and cook until browned on the second side, about 5 minutes more. Transfer to a rimmed plate. Reduce the heat to medium and add the onion and garlic to the pan. Cook, stirring, until the onion is softened and lightly browned, about 5 minutes. Pour in the hard cider and chicken stock and use a wooden spoon to scrape any browned bits from the bottom of the pan.

> Add the parsnips, carrots, and thyme sprigs to the pot, followed by the chicken and

RECIPE CONTINUES ↘

pancetta. Cover the pot, transfer to the oven, and cook for 30 minutes.

> Remove from the oven and use a slotted spoon to transfer the chicken, parsnips, and carrots to a high-sided serving dish. Bring the braising liquid to a boil and season to taste with salt and pepper. Add the Brussels sprouts and cook until tender, about 5 minutes, then pour the braising juices and sprouts over the chicken, parsnips, and carrots. Serve immediately.

THREE WAYS WITH BEANS

Maine Truck Stop Baked Beans

Serves 6 to 8

---

2 cups (1 pound) dried Yellow Eye or navy beans

1/2 cup molasses

1/3 cup maple syrup

1/3 cup ketchup

2 teaspoons kosher salt

2 teaspoons dry mustard powder

1/2 teaspoon freshly ground black pepper

1 small onion, peeled and diced

1/4 pound salt pork or pancetta, diced

ONE OF MY FAVORITE PLACES in Maine is a truck stop called Dysart's, off Interstate 95 in Bangor, where my wife was raised. It offers amenities for long-haul truckers like hot showers, a mechanic shop, and a restaurant, which has a room reserved exclusively for truck drivers. Dysart's has little competition—there aren't many good places to stop between Bangor and Canada—and they could easily serve shitty food and still have customers. Instead, they buy beef and pork raised nearby and local potatoes, apples, maple syrup, and dried beans.

Dysart's serves baked beans all day. They're made according to someone's grandmother's recipe, and I have a hard time resisting a bowlful when I'm there, no matter the time of day.

Maine lore says that the closer you live to Boston, the more likely you are to make baked beans with navy beans than with the varieties more popular in rural Maine, such as Jacob's Cattle or Yellow Eye. I'm not sure how much geography has to do with it, but Mainers are on to something—Yellow Eye beans are especially creamy, with thin skins, and they're my choice if you can find them. (If you're looking for a source for some of the best dried beans in America, check out ranchogordo.com.)

Tradition dictates that you pair your beans with hot dogs, and that's never wrong—salty franks and sweet baked beans are a classic and delicious combination. I also like the beans the next day, cold, sandwiched between two slices of bread, the sort of carb-on-carb specialty that betrays my Yankee roots.

I make my beans with salt pork, but if you can't find it, pancetta is a good substitute. If you don't own a bean pot—I found mine, a real McCoy, in a pile of trash outside a house in San Francisco—use a Dutch oven or other heavy pot. Cooked baked beans can be frozen; cool completely, then spoon into plastic storage bags and lay flat in the freezer. They'll keep for up to three months. Note that for this recipe, the beans need to be soaked overnight.

> Put the beans in a bowl and add cold water to cover by a few inches. Soak overnight, then drain and transfer to a

RECIPE CONTINUES ↘

large saucepan or Dutch oven and add fresh water to cover. Preheat the oven to 250°F. Bring the beans to a boil over high heat, reduce the heat so the water is simmering, and simmer until the beans are tender and the skins peel back when you blow on a spoonful, about 45 minutes to an hour. Drain, reserving the bean cooking liquid, and transfer the beans to a bean pot or small Dutch oven.

> In a small bowl, stir together the molasses, maple syrup, ketchup, salt, mustard powder, and black pepper. Pour over the beans, then stir in the onion and salt pork. Add about 2 to 3 cups of the bean cooking water to the beans (the water should just cover the beans, not swamp them—the beans should look like they're sitting in a bathtub) and stir well to mix.

> Cover the pot and transfer to the oven. Cook until the beans are completely tender, about 3 hours. Uncover the pot, increase the oven temperature to 325°F, and continue cooking about 45 minutes more, until the cooking liquid has reduced and a crust has formed on the surface of the beans.

> Stir the beans and season to taste with additional salt. Depending on the dimensions of the pot you use, your beans may be more soupy or less so. If you want to thicken the beans, remove 1 cup of the cooked beans and transfer to a bowl. Mash with a potato masher, then return the mashed beans to the pot and stir to combine. If they're too thick, add a bit more of the reserved bean cooking liquid to thin them.

> The beans can be eaten right away or cooled to room temperature and refrigerated—eat them cold or reheat in a low oven or in a saucepan on the stovetop over low heat.

Beans *and* Greens

Serves 6 to 8

1 pound dried cannellini or corona beans

1 to 2 tablespoons kosher salt

4 pounds greens, preferably a mix of escarole, broccoli rabe, Swiss chard, spinach, kale, and dandelion greens, stemmed and washed

1 cup plus 2 tablespoons olive oil

8 cloves garlic, peeled (4 cloves thinly sliced, 4 cloves left whole)

3 oil-packed anchovy fillets

1 teaspoon red pepper flakes

Zest and juice of 1 large lemon

1 cup fresh bread crumbs

MY FRIEND LIZA SHAW is a fabulous cook who really knows her way around a pot of beans. This might sound like a dubious distinction unless you like beans as much as I do, and I really owe Liza a huge debt of gratitude for teaching me her method, which involves sautéing the cooked beans in a generous quantity of olive oil and then ladling in some of the bean cooking liquid, which emulsifies with the olive oil and the starch from the beans into a sort of super-sauce, creamy and deeply flavored. Sounds simple, but it's a trick for the ages.

Prepared like this, the beans are good enough to eat without any other additions, maybe topped with bread crumbs and some grated Parmigiano. But when combined with winter greens, the beans become a sort of peasant power food, rich and satisfying.

This makes a large batch, but I think if you're going to go to the trouble of cooking dried beans, you might as well make a good quantity (and no, you can't use canned beans; the bean cooking liquid is integral to the recipe). And every time I considered scaling down this large recipe, friends protested, agreeing with my assertion that these beans can be eaten three meals a day.

I like to use a combination of different leafy greens in this recipe; escarole, broccoli rabe, dandelion greens, kale, and Swiss chard are all good. Four pounds of greens will look, in Liza's words, "like an insane amount," but they cook down tremendously. However, I usually buy the greens the same day I make this recipe because I don't have refrigerator space to store them. If you want to make this a vegan dish, omit the anchovy fillets. Note that the beans must be soaked overnight.

> Put the dried beans in a large Dutch oven or heavy-bottomed pot and add cold water to cover by several inches. Soak overnight. The next day, add more water as needed to the pot so the beans are covered by several inches. Bring to a boil over medium-high heat, then reduce heat and simmer until the beans are tender, about 1½ to 2 hours. Periodically check the water level of the beans; they should be covered

RECIPE CONTINUES ↘

by several inches of water throughout the cooking. Add more boiling water to the pot as needed (I keep a water-filled teakettle on the adjacent burner, turning it on and topping off the beans as needed).

> The beans are done when you pull five from the pot and all are tender—as Liza says, if you're chewing a bean and wondering if it's cooked enough, it's not. When the beans are tender, remove them from the heat but do not drain. Season the cooking water with salt. The exact amount you'll use will depend on how much cooking liquid is in the pot, so begin with a small amount and continue adding until the liquid tastes very well seasoned, just this side of salty. Let the beans cool in the cooking liquid. The beans can be made up to 2 days in advance; once cool, cover and transfer to the refrigerator.

> Meanwhile, bring a large pot of salted water to a boil. Set a large ice bath nearby. Working in batches by type of greens, blanch the greens until they wilt and are tender, about

2 minutes (slightly longer for broccoli rabe). Remove from the water with tongs or a spider and transfer to the ice bath. Once cool, transfer to a rimmed baking sheet. When all the greens have been cooked, grab fistfuls of greens and, working over the sink or a bowl, squeeze them to extract the maximum amount of liquid. Transfer to a cutting board. Coarsely chop and transfer to a bowl.

> In a small frying pan, heat ½ cup of the olive oil with the sliced garlic, the anchovy fillets, and ½ teaspoon of the red pepper flakes. Cook over medium-low heat until the garlic begins to sizzle but does not brown, using the back of a spoon to mash the anchovy fillets to a paste. Remove from the heat, stir in half the lemon zest, pour the mixture over the greens, and stir to coat.

> Return the frying pan to medium heat and add 2 tablespoons of the olive oil. Add the bread crumbs and stir to coat with oil. Toast the bread crumbs, stirring, until dark golden brown and crunchy, about 5 to 6 minutes. Season with salt and set aside.

> In a Dutch oven or heavy pot, heat the remaining ½ cup olive oil over medium-high heat and add the whole garlic cloves and the remaining teaspoon of red pepper flakes (or less, if you prefer a milder dish). When the garlic begins to sizzle, add half of the cooked beans (but not their liquid) and fry, stirring, until the skins begin to split slightly, about 2 minutes. Add a ladleful of the cooking liquid, increase the heat to high, and cook, stirring, until the liquid begins to boil and a creamy, emulsified sauce forms.

> Add the remaining beans and some more cooking liquid; the beans should be quite saucy. Stir in the greens, add more bean cooking liquid as necessary to maintain their sauciness, and cook until the greens are heated through. Remove from the heat and stir in the remaining lemon zest and the lemon juice to taste. Season to taste with additional salt. Top with the bread crumbs and serve warm.

Basic Black Beans

Serves 6

1 pound dried black beans

2 teaspoons kosher salt

2 tablespoons extra-virgin olive oil

½ cup diced yellow or white onion

OFTEN COOK A POT of black beans on Sunday afternoon; this is one bean recipe in which the beans don't need overnight soaking, so it doesn't require the advanced planning of the other dried-bean recipes in this book. When they're soft and saucy, I scoop them onto rice and eat them for supper, dressed up with cubes of avocado, crumbled queso fresco, chopped cilantro, and hot sauce (this is another meal that my kids will customize to their taste, like the vermicelli on page 143 and the Tortilla Soup on page 112).

A pound of dried beans makes a big pot (and costs almost nothing), so there's plenty left over for the rest of the week. I reheat a mugful for a quick working lunch, spoon them onto warmed tortillas as a snack for my boys, top a bowlful with some coconut cream and grated lime zest, or serve them alongside steak or grilled fish. As with baked beans (page 158), they're also good on toast. Cooked beans can be frozen; cool completely, then spoon into plastic storage bags and lay flat in the freezer. They'll keep for up to three months.

> Rinse the beans and pick out any stones or broken beans and discard. Transfer the beans to a large heavy pot and add water to cover by 2 inches. Add the salt, cover the pot partially, and turn the heat to medium. Cook the beans, partially covered, for 20 minutes (at the 20-minute point, the liquid should be boiling; if it isn't, turn up the heat slightly until it is).

> Reduce the heat to low and cook the beans, still partially covered, until just tender, about 1 hour more. Uncover the beans and give them a stir; if the water level is low, add more hot water so the beans are covered by about an inch. In a small frying pan, heat the olive oil over medium heat. Add the onion and a pinch of salt and cook, stirring, until translucent, about 6 minutes. Pour the onions and oil into the pot of beans.

> Increase the heat to medium high and cook, uncovered, until the beans are very tender and the liquid is thick, about 20 minutes more. Season to taste with additional salt.

Chicken *and* Herbed Dumplings

Serves 6

1 (3- to 4-pound) chicken

1 large onion, peeled and cut into large chunks

2 sprigs fresh parsley plus ½ cup minced fresh parsley leaves

2 sprigs fresh thyme plus 1 teaspoon chopped fresh thyme leaves

Kosher salt

8 tablespoons unsalted butter

1 small onion, peeled and finely diced

20 cremini or button mushrooms, stemmed and quartered

2 medium carrots, peeled and finely diced (about 1 cup)

½ cup flour

Freshly ground black pepper

¼ cup heavy cream

THE BEST THING about a cooking repertoire is that it's dynamic, built from recipes that you collect throughout your life—dishes you learn from friends, order at restaurants, or try when traveling and want to replicate at home.

I learned to make chicken and dumplings from my Puerto Rican friend Eduardo, an exceptional cook. Other dumpling recipes often contain butter, but Eduardo's are more like herby sponge cakes, fluffy clouds that float on top of the gravy.

It's more economical to make this with a whole chicken; quickly poaching it gives you both the stock and the meat you need for this recipe. The technique is the same as for the Tortilla Soup on page 112. If you don't want to hack up the chicken yourself, ask someone at the meat counter to do it for you, but don't buy chicken pieces, because you will need the backbone and wings for the stock. If you're short on time, shredded cooked chicken and prepared chicken stock are fine shortcuts.

FOR THE DUMPLINGS:

1½ cups all-purpose flour

2 teaspoons baking powder

1 teaspoon kosher salt

1 teaspoon sugar

1 cup whole milk

1 egg, beaten

¼ cup minced soft herbs, such as tarragon, chervil, chives, or parsley

2 green onions, thinly sliced

> With a sharp knife, remove the chicken wings and set aside. Cut the chicken into 2 thighs, 2 legs, and 2 breasts and remove the skin from each piece. Cut each breast crosswise in half. With a cleaver, cut the backbone into 2-inch pieces and separate each wing in two. Heat a Dutch oven or heavy-bottomed pot over medium-high heat and add the chicken backbone and wing pieces (and the neck, if you have it) and the large onion chunks. Cook, stirring, until the chicken pieces begin to brown, about 4 minutes. Pour in ¼ cup of water, reduce heat to low, add the parsley

RECIPE CONTINUES ↘

and thyme sprigs, cover, and cook for 20 minutes.

> Increase the heat to medium high and add 6 cups of hot water (from the tap is fine), the skinned chicken breasts, thighs, and drumsticks, and 1 teaspoon of salt. Bring to a boil, reduce the heat so the liquid is simmering, cover the pot partially, and simmer until the chicken pieces are just cooked through, about 20 minutes. With a slotted spoon or tongs, remove the chicken pieces from the pot and transfer to a rimmed plate or baking sheet. When cool enough to handle, pull the chicken meat from the bones and shred; you should have about 4 cups of meat. Strain the chicken stock through a fine-mesh strainer into a bowl and discard the bones, onion, and herbs; you should have about 6 cups of chicken stock.

> Rinse out the Dutch oven and place over medium heat. Add the butter, and when the butter has melted, add the finely diced onion, mushrooms, and carrots. Sauté until the vegetables are just tender but not brown, about 6 minutes. Sprinkle the flour over the vegetables and cook, stirring, for 2 minutes. Pour in 5 cups of the reserved chicken stock (save any remaining stock for another use), bring to a simmer, and cook until the gravy thickens, 2 to 3 minutes. Stir in the chopped parsley and chopped thyme and 3 cups of the shredded chicken (save the remaining chicken for another use) and season to taste with salt and pepper. Turn off the heat and stir in the heavy cream.

> **MAKE THE DUMPLINGS:** In a medium bowl, whisk together the flour, baking powder, salt, and sugar. Whisk the milk and eggs together, then pour into the dry ingredients. Add the herbs and green onions and stir with a spoon until well combined.

> Return the pot to medium-low heat and cook, stirring, until the gravy begins to bubble. With a tablespoon, drop spoonfuls of the dumpling batter onto the surface of the chicken mixture. Repeat until all of the batter has been used; the dumplings will be close together, even touching. Reduce the heat to low, cover, and cook for 5 minutes.

Uncover and use a spoon to flip each dumpling; they will have puffed dramatically and should be cooked through on the bottom but still raw-looking on top. Cover and cook 5 minutes more, until the dumplings are cooked through (you can use a spoon to cut a dumpling in half to check; it should be fluffy throughout). Remove from the heat.

> To serve, spoon a few dumplings into each bowl, then spoon some of the chicken mixture over and around the dumplings. Serve hot.

———

Note · *The chicken filling here can also be used to make a chicken potpie. If I'm doing that, I like to stir some frozen peas into the mixture when I add the parsley, thyme, and heavy cream. Transfer the filling to a casserole dish and top with pastry, like the dough used for the onion tart on page 48, rolled to a thickness of about a quarter inch. Cut a few vents in the pastry to allow steam to escape and bake at 375°F until the pastry is golden brown, about 50 minutes.*

Candy Pork

Serves 6

8 ounces palm sugar, finely chopped (dark brown sugar can be substituted)

¾ cup fish sauce

3 tablespoons canola oil

4 pounds boneless pork shoulder, cut into 2-inch-by-3-inch chunks

Kosher salt and freshly ground black pepper

1 cup thinly sliced shallots

One 2-inch-by-1-inch piece fresh ginger, peeled and julienned

2 cloves garlic, peeled and crushed

2 to 3 Thai chilies (substitute 1 serrano chile), stemmed and crushed

3 cups coconut water

THIS IS WHAT MY KIDS call this recipe. Large chunks of pork shoulder are braised in a Vietnamese-style caramel sauce (made from a combination of fish sauce and palm sugar) that's laced with Thai chilies, ginger, garlic, and shallots. The liquid in this braise is coconut water (not coconut milk), a trick I learned from chef Charles Phan when I was working with him on his first cookbook, *Vietnamese Home Cooking*.

The pork emerges from the oven lacquered, tender, and sweet. Serve the fork-tender meat with plenty of rice and some sautéed pea shoots or greens.

> Put the palm sugar in a medium heavy-bottomed saucepan over medium-low heat. Cook until the sugar melts, about 8 to 10 minutes, stirring frequently so the sugar doesn't scorch. When the sugar is smooth and completely melted, remove the pan from the heat and slowly stir in the fish sauce. The mixture may seize; if it does, return it to low heat and continue stirring until smooth.

> Preheat the oven to 300°F. In a large Dutch oven over high heat, heat the canola oil. Season the pork pieces on all sides with salt and pepper. When the oil is hot, add some of the pieces of pork and sear until well browned on all sides, about 8 minutes. Transfer to a rimmed baking sheet and repeat with the remaining pork. When all the pork has been browned, reduce the heat to medium and add the shallots. Cook, stirring, until the shallots are softened, about 2 minutes, then add the ginger, garlic, and chilies and cook 1 minute more. Return the pork and any accumulated juices to the pot and add the caramel sauce and coconut water. The pieces of meat should poke up above the level of the liquid; if they're completely submerged, transfer the meat and liquid to a different pot. Bring to a boil, then reduce the heat so the liquid is simmering. Cover the pot and transfer to the oven.

> After 15 minutes of cooking, uncover the pot; the liquid should be simmering gently. If it's bubbling too vigorously, reduce the oven temperature to 275°F. Cook for 70 minutes—the meat

should be tender but not falling apart. Uncover the pot and continue cooking for 30 minutes more, until the exposed bits of pork are caramelized and the meat is tender. Remove from the oven and serve with steamed rice.

Sweets

Apricot-Nectarine Crisp

Serves 6

1 cup plus 2 tablespoons all-purpose flour

½ cup finely chopped walnuts

½ cup plus 2 tablespoons granulated sugar

¼ cup packed dark brown sugar

¼ teaspoon ground cinnamon

8 tablespoons unsalted butter, melted and cooled to room temperature, plus more for the pan

2½ pounds apricots and nectarines; apricots pitted and quartered, nectarines pitted and sliced

1 teaspoon tapioca

Vanilla ice cream, for serving (optional)

LIKE SO MANY SIMPLE THINGS, fruit crisps are easy to get wrong. The problem is usually with the topping, which can be so fine it sinks into the fruit or else padded with unnecessary ingredients, like oats or, even worse, lemon zest. Mine is straightforward: just sugar, walnuts, and flour drizzled with melted butter. Using melted butter causes the mixture to form into craggy clumps, a nutty, rich gravel to spread over the fruit.

At once sweet and tart, fuzzy like babies' cheeks, Blenheim apricots become silky and jammy when baked. I add in some nectarines—you can vary the proportion of fruit to your own taste, but I like a mixture that's two-thirds apricots, one-third nectarines by weight.

If apricots aren't in season or aren't available where you live, you can use any seasonal fruit you prefer. A handful of raspberries or pitted cherries would be a nice addition to the apricots and nectarines. As summer wears on, this crisp can be made with peaches or plums, and when stone-fruit season finally comes to an end, there are apples to look forward to.

Bake the crisp until the topping is a deep brown and the fruit juices look thick and sticky.

———

> Preheat the oven to 375°F. In a large bowl, whisk together the flour, walnuts, ¼ cup of the granulated sugar, the brown sugar, and the cinnamon. Drizzle the butter over and stir with a fork until the mixture clumps together; break up any large chunks with your fingers, but don't break it up too much.

> In a large bowl, combine the fruit, the remaining 6 tablespoons granulated sugar, and the tapioca. Mix well to combine and let stand 10 minutes. Butter a 2-quart gratin or casserole dish. Transfer the fruit to the prepared dish and spread in a thick, even layer. Top with the crumble mixture, distributing evenly. Place on a rimmed baking sheet to catch any bubble-over and transfer to the oven. Bake until the bubbling juices look thick and the topping is well browned, about 1 hour. Remove from the oven and transfer to a wire rack to cool. Serve warm or at room temperature, accompanied by a scoop of ice cream.

Sour Cherry Hand Pies

Makes 8 hand pies

2 cups all-purpose flour

½ teaspoon fine sea salt

1 cup cold unsalted butter, cut into 1-inch pieces

3½ cups pitted sour cherries

¾ cup sugar

3 tablespoons cornstarch

1 tablespoon lemon juice

1 teaspoon lemon zest

1 egg

1 teaspoon water

Sanding sugar or raw sugar, for sprinkling on top

A FEW YEARS BACK, I took a summer trip to Michigan with some friends. I am a huge fan of cherry pie, and knowing Michigan is cherry country, we timed our visit to coincide with the harvest. I made a vacation rule: We'd buy every cherry pie we encountered along the way in a quest to find the very best the state had to offer.

After a couple of days, the trunk of the car was filled with pies in various stages of destruction—sad evidence that our epic tasting had been a disappointment. Many of the pies had gluey, overly thickened fillings, and others had pale, flavorless crusts made with shortening only—all flake, no flavor. Some were even made with Bing cherries instead of a sour variety, so they lacked the tartness I craved.

If only I'd found these little hand pies at some Michigan roadside stand! The half-moons are made with rough puff pastry, a cheater's version of puff pastry that is flaky and light but takes a fraction of the work required for traditional puff pastry. As for the filling, it's all about the fruit, which I sweeten a bit but not so much as to obliterate what's awesome about sour cherries, their beguiling tartness.

If you can't find fresh or frozen sour cherries, substitute an equal amount of canned sour cherries. They're usually packed in heavy syrup and should be drained and rinsed of all syrup before you start. Or, if you want to veer in a completely different direction, see my note on page 179 for a blueberry variation.

> Fill a 1-cup measuring cup with ice and add water. Combine the flour and salt in a large bowl. Add the butter and toss to coat with flour. Using a pastry cutter, cut the butter into the flour until the pieces of butter are about half an inch. Add ½ cup of the ice water and continue cutting the butter into the flour until a shaggy dough forms.

> Turn out onto a lightly floured work surface. The dough will look very rough at this point, hardly like dough at all. This is okay. Pat into a rectangle, then use a lightly floured rolling pin to roll into a ragged 6-inch-by-18-inch rectangle.

RECIPE CONTINUES ↘

> With a bench scraper, fold the short ends toward each other so they meet in the middle. Fold one half over the other half to make a 4-inch-by-6-inch rectangle. Turn the dough so that the fold is on the right. Roll into a 6-inch-by-18-inch rectangle and repeat the folding technique, then wrap tightly in plastic and refrigerate for 20 minutes.

> Return the dough to the lightly floured work surface and position so the fold is on the right. Roll into a 6-inch-by-18-inch rectangle and fold the dough again as directed above, flouring the dough to prevent sticking. At this point the dough should look smooth, with visible tongues of butter. Wrap tightly with plastic wrap and refrigerate at least 2 hours or overnight.

> In a medium saucepan over medium heat, combine the cherries, sugar, cornstarch, lemon juice, and lemon zest. Stir to combine, then cook, stirring occasionally, until the cherries release their juices and the juices thicken, about 10 minutes. Transfer to a bowl and let cool to room temperature, then transfer to the refrigerator; it will thicken as it cools.

> Line a rimmed baking sheet with a silicone baking mat or parchment paper. On a lightly floured work surface with a lightly floured rolling pin, roll the dough into a large rectangle about ¼ inch thick. With a 5-inch round cutter, stamp out 8 rounds from the dough (save the scraps, which can be dusted with cinnamon sugar or grated cheese and baked as a snack). In a small bowl, whisk together the egg and water.

> With a pastry brush, paint egg wash around the border of each circle of dough (transfer the remaining egg wash to a lidded container and refrigerate).

> Spoon some of the cold cherry filling into the center of a round of dough, fold over to form a half-moon, then crimp the edges to seal (do not overfill the turnovers; they'll be more likely to leak). Transfer to the prepared baking sheet. Repeat with the remaining dough and filling.

> When all the hand pies have been formed, transfer the pies (still on the baking sheet) to the freezer and freeze until solid, at least 2 hours or overnight.

> Preheat the oven to 400°F. Remove the pies from the freezer and use a pastry brush to brush the tops with the reserved egg wash. Sprinkle with sanding sugar. Transfer to the oven and bake until the pastry is puffed and deep golden brown, about 25 to 30 minutes. Remove from the oven and let cool slightly, then use a spatula to transfer the pies to a wire cooling rack and let cool completely. The pies are best eaten the same day they are made.

Swapping blueberries for sour cherries: As much as I love sour cherries, they break my heart. Their short season and limited availability make them the elusive white whale of the fruit world. Happily, these hand pies are also very delicious made with blueberries.

For a blueberry filling, combine 2 cups fresh or frozen blueberries, 3 tablespoons sugar, 1 tablespoon plus 1 teaspoon cornstarch (if using frozen blueberries, increase to 1½ tablespoons), 1 tablespoon lemon juice, 1 teaspoon lemon zest, ¼ teaspoon ground cinnamon, a pinch of fine sea salt, and 1 tablespoon water.

Stir to combine, then cook, stirring occasionally, until the blueberries release their juices and the juices thicken, about 10 minutes. Transfer to a bowl and refrigerate until cold; it will thicken as it cools. Fill and bake as described on the facing page.

Strawberry Sundaes

Makes 4 to 6 sundaes

FOR THE ICE CREAM:

1¾ cups heavy cream

¾ cup 1 or 2 percent milk

¾ cup sugar

4 egg yolks

½ teaspoon kosher salt

2 cups finely diced fresh ripe strawberries

1 teaspoon vanilla extract

FOR THE COMPOTE:

2 cups sliced fresh ripe strawberries

2 tablespoons sugar

1 teaspoon lemon juice

FOR THE WHIPPED CREAM:

1 cup chilled heavy cream

1 tablespoon confectioners' sugar

½ teaspoon vanilla extract

IT'S HARD TO DETHRONE the banana split as the best ice cream sundae of all time, but this strawberry version comes close. You don't have to make the ice cream (Häagen-Dazs is my store-bought strawberry ice cream of choice), though if you do, the sundaes will be that much better.

_____

> MAKE THE ICE CREAM: In a medium saucepan over medium heat, whisk together the heavy cream, milk, and ¼ cup of the sugar. Cook, whisking, until bubbles begin to form at the edge of the pan.

> In a medium bowl, whisk together the egg yolks and ¼ cup of the sugar until well combined. Whisking constantly, pour in half of the hot cream mixture and continue whisking until mixed. Pour the egg-yolk mixture into the saucepan with the remaining hot cream mixture, add the salt, and cook over medium heat, stirring constantly with a rubber spatula or wooden spoon, until the custard thickens enough to coat the back of a spoon, about 5 minutes. Remove from the heat.

> Put the strawberries and remaining ¼ cup sugar in a medium bowl. With a potato masher or the back of a fork, coarsely mash the berries. Pour the custard through a fine-mesh sieve into the bowl containing the berries and stir to combine. Set the bowl in an ice bath and let stand, stirring occasionally, until cool. Wrap the bowl tightly with plastic wrap and refrigerate overnight. Stir in the vanilla extract and churn in an ice cream maker according to manufacturer's instructions.

> MAKE THE COMPOTE: In a medium saucepan, combine the strawberries, sugar, and lemon juice. Cook over medium-low heat, stirring occasionally, until the strawberries begin to soften and release their juices, about 5 minutes. Remove from the heat and let cool.

> When you're ready to assemble the sundaes, make the whipped cream. In the bowl of an electric mixer fitted with the whisk attachment (or in a large bowl with a handheld mixer or whisk) combine the cream, confectioners' sugar,

and vanilla extract. Beat on medium speed until the cream holds soft peaks (do not overwhip the cream; it should be cloudlike).

> To assemble each sundae, scoop a small amount of compote into the bottom of a parfait glass. Top with a scoop of strawberry ice cream, another spoonful of compote, and a generous amount of whipped cream. Serve right away.

FOR THE MERINGUE:

1 cup superfine sugar

1 tablespoon cornstarch

3 large eggs

Pinch kosher salt

1 teaspoon lemon juice

1 teaspoon vanilla extract

FOR THE LIME CURD:

¼ cup sugar

¼ cup lime juice

Zest of 1 lime

1 tablespoon unsalted butter, cut into ½-inch cubes

....

1 cup heavy cream

1 tablespoon confectioners' sugar

4 cups blue berries, such as blueberries, blackberries, mulberries, or a mixture

Pavlova *with* Lime Curd *and* Blue Berries

I T'S A MINOR GOAL OF MINE to someday have something named after me, and given my deep love of sweets, it makes sense it would be a dessert, not a basketball stadium or a hospital wing. What I love most about pavlova—a dessert named for a Russian ballerina, Anna Pavlova—is its contrasting flavors and textures. The meringue has a crisp crust and a soft, marshmallow-like interior; here its sweetness is offset by tart lime curd and billows of softly whipped cream.

In summertime, I like to top the pavlova with an assortment of blue berries (another striking contrast to the pale meringue), though you could substitute strawberries or raspberries or a mixture. In winter, you can top your pavlova with tropical fruit (I especially like mango) or an assortment of sliced citrus (I like a mixture of orange and grapefruit supremes and kumquats, which I slice into rounds, peel and all, and poach briefly in sugar syrup), or cranberries cooked in sugar syrup just until they begin to pop.

The curd can be made a few days ahead and refrigerated, but don't top the pavlova until just before serving or it will become soggy. Baked meringue can be frozen. Let cool completely, then wrap in plastic (the challenge for me is to avoid crushing it in my often-overstuffed freezer). When you're ready to serve, remove from the freezer and unwrap right away, before water condenses on the plastic and sogs out the meringue.

> MAKE THE MERINGUE: Preheat the oven to 250°F and line a rimmed baking sheet with a silicone baking mat or parchment. In a medium bowl, whisk together the sugar and cornstarch. Separate the eggs. Set the yolks aside for the lime curd.

Put the egg whites and salt in the bowl of an electric mixer fitted with the whisk attachment (or in a large bowl with a handheld mixer). Mix on medium speed until the whites hold soft peaks, then add 3 tablespoons of cold

RECIPE CONTINUES ↘

water and continue beating until the whites again hold soft peaks. Increase the speed to medium high and add the sugar and cornstarch mixture 1 tablespoon at a time. When all the sugar has been added, beat 1 minute more.

> Add the lemon juice and vanilla, increase the speed to high, and continue to beat the egg whites until they hold stiff, glossy peaks, 5 minutes more. Transfer the meringue to the prepared pan and, using an offset spatula or the back of a spoon, gently spread into a circle about 8 inches wide, slightly higher on the sides and with a slight depression in the center. If you prefer, you can make individual meringues; prepare two baking sheets, then spoon 4 equal-size mounds of meringue onto each of the baking sheets. The baking time is the same.

> Bake the meringue until pale golden, about 45 minutes. The meringue will have a crust on the exterior but still be soft inside. Turn the oven off, crack the oven door slightly (stick a wooden spoon in the oven door to keep it propped open), and let the meringue sit in the oven for 1 hour. Remove from the oven and let cool completely. Once cool, run a spatula under the meringue to free it from the silicone baking mat or parchment and transfer to a large plate. The meringue is best made the same day you plan to eat it. (If you want to make it ahead of time, freeze it; it eventually gets soggy at room temperature.)

> WHILE THE MERINGUE COOKS, MAKE THE LIME CURD: In a medium nonreactive bowl, whisk together the reserved egg yolks, sugar, and lime juice. Place the bowl over a saucepan of simmering water (ensuring the bottom of the bowl does not touch the water) and whisk vigorously and constantly until the mixture is thick enough to coat the back of a spoon, about 5 to 8 minutes. Remove from the heat and whisk in the lime zest and butter. Press a sheet of plastic wrap directly on the surface of the curd (this prevents a skin from forming) and refrigerate until cold. The lime curd can be made up to 2 days in advance; if you make the curd

before the meringue, be sure to reserve the egg whites for the meringue. If you prefer lemon curd to lime, substitute lemon juice and zest for the lime juice and zest; the method remains the same.

> ASSEMBLE THE PAVLOVA: In an electric mixer fitted with the whisk attachment (or in a large bowl with a handheld mixer) beat the cream and confectioners' sugar on high speed until it holds soft peaks. With a rubber spatula, fold a third of the whipped cream into the lime curd to lighten it. Spread the lime curd onto the meringue base, leaving a 1-inch border. Top with the remaining whipped cream. Arrange the berries on top of the cream. The pavlova is best eaten right after it's assembled but can be prepared up to an hour before you plan to serve it and refrigerated.

Coconut Cream Party Cake

Makes one 8 inch layer cake

FOR THE COCONUT
PASTRY CREAM:

2 cups whole milk

**2 cups finely shredded
sweetened flaked coconut**

1 vanilla bean

2 large eggs

½ cup sugar

3 tablespoons flour

**3 tablespoons unsalted butter,
at room temperature**

INGREDIENT LIST CONTINUES ⟍

THERE'S A LINE FROM a Bonnie Raitt song that I love, when she sings that in her "sweet dreams" she's in a bar on her birthday, "drinking salty margaritas with Fernando."

Well, I like salty margaritas, but in my sweet dreams it's my birthday and someone has baked me this cake.

I have spent a lot of my life trying to develop a recipe for the ultimate yellow cake, one that tastes like it came from a mix. This is a strange goal, I realize, to attempt a homemade version that replicates something you can get out of a box, but I think a lot of us have nostalgia for cakes with that distinctive flavor and delicate crumb. It's the taste of childhood birthday parties, the specific flavor of joy.

I'm happy to say that after years of fine-tuning, this is the recipe that I (and maybe you?) have been waiting for. It's incredibly tender, rich but not dense, and tastes strongly of vanilla.

Coconut pastry cream is sandwiched between the layers and then the cake is frosted with a silky, lighter-than-average ganache that's made with water instead of cream (an idea for which I must give the celebrated cookbook author David Lebovitz credit). It's like a Mounds bar in cake form, and it makes people so happy when you trot this masterpiece out. Said one of my recipe testers, "I was blown away by this recipe. The tender crumb on the cake, the rich but light frosting, the easy pastry cream—I could not get enough."

> MAKE THE PASTRY CREAM:
In a medium saucepan over medium-high heat, combine the milk and coconut. Split the vanilla bean lengthwise and use the tip of a knife to scrape out the seeds; add both seeds and pod to the milk mixture. Bring mixture to a gentle simmer, stirring occasionally.

> In a medium bowl, whisk together the eggs, sugar, and flour. While whisking, drizzle about a third of the hot milk mixture into the egg mixture, then slowly whisk the egg-milk mixture back into the saucepan. Cook over medium-high heat, whisking, until the pastry cream thickens and begins to bubble, 4 to 5 minutes.

RECIPE CONTINUES ⟍

FOR THE CAKE:

2¼ cups cake flour

1¼ teaspoons baking powder

¼ teaspoon baking soda

½ teaspoon kosher salt

½ cup milk, at room temperature

⅓ cup sour cream, at room temperature

1 cup unsalted butter, at room temperature

1¾ cups granulated sugar

1 tablespoon vanilla extract

3 large eggs, at room temperature

2 large egg yolks, at room temperature

FOR THE GANACHE:

4 ounces good-quality milk chocolate, chopped

4 ounces good-quality semisweet chocolate (64 percent), chopped

⅓ cup water

10 tablespoons unsalted butter, cubed

....

¼ cup unsweetened large-flake coconut, lightly toasted, for garnish (optional)

Remove from heat, stir in butter, and remove and discard the vanilla bean. Transfer to a bowl and let cool slightly, then cover the bowl with a sheet of plastic wrap, pressing it down directly on the surface of the pastry cream to prevent a skin from forming. Refrigerate until cold, about 3 hours. The pastry cream can be made ahead and kept, refrigerated, for 2 days.

> MAKE THE CAKE: Preheat the oven to 350°F and arrange a rack in the center of the oven. Grease two 8-inch round cake pans, line the bottom of each pan with parchment paper, and grease and flour the parchment. Sift the flour, baking powder, baking soda, and salt together into a bowl. In a second bowl, stir together the milk and sour cream.

> In the bowl of an electric mixer fitted with the paddle attachment, beat the butter and sugar on medium speed until soft and fluffy, about 4 to 5 minutes. Mix in the vanilla. Add the eggs, one at a time, mixing between each addition, then add the egg yolks and mix just until combined, scraping down the sides of the bowl with a rubber spatula as needed.

> Add a third of the dry ingredients to the batter and mix just until combined, scraping down the sides of the bowl as needed. Add half the milk–sour cream mixture and mix. Add half the remaining dry ingredients, mixing just until combined. Add the remaining milk–sour cream mixture and beat just until combined, then add the remaining dry ingredients and mix just until combined. Remove the bowl from the mixer and, with a rubber spatula, scrape down the sides of the bowl and give the batter one final stir.

> Divide the batter evenly between the prepared cake pans, transfer them to the oven, and bake for 30 to 35 minutes, until golden around the edges and beginning to pull away from the sides of the pan; a toothpick inserted in the center should come out clean. Let cool in the pan on a wire rack for 10 minutes, then gently turn the layers out, peel off the parchment, and let cool completely. The

cakes can be made up to 1 day in advance. When the layers are cool, tightly wrap them in plastic wrap and refrigerate until ready to use. The cooled layers can also be tightly wrapped and frozen for up to a month.

> While the cake bakes and cools, make the ganache: In a medium bowl, combine the chocolate and water. Set the bowl over a pan of simmering water, making sure that the bottom of the bowl does not touch the water, and heat, stirring occasionally, until the chocolate has melted and the mixture is smooth. Remove from the heat and whisk in the butter, then transfer to the refrigerator and chill, stirring occasionally, until the ganache has the texture of peanut butter, about 20 minutes (alternatively, you can let the ganache cool at room temperature until it reaches the desired consistency, about 1 hour; the refrigerator just speeds up the process). The ganache can be made ahead and refrigerated; let come to room temperature before using.

> **TO ASSEMBLE THE CAKE:** With a large serrated knife, cut each cake layer in half lengthwise to create 2 thin layers (Note: It can be easier to cut a chilled—or even frozen—cake.) Set a cake layer on a cake stand or large plate. Spoon a third of the chilled pastry cream onto the layer and, with an offset spatula, spread into a thin, even layer, stopping just short of the edges. Top with a second layer of cake, top the cake with half the remaining pastry cream, and spread it into an even layer. Repeat this layering until you've used all the pastry cream and all 4 cake layers, leaving the final layer of cake plain.

> Spoon half of the ganache frosting on top of the cake and, with an offset spatula, spread over the top and sides of the cake in a thin layer. Spoon the remaining frosting on the top of the cake and spread evenly over the cake. Press the toasted coconut, if using, onto the sides of the cake. Refrigerate the cake at least 15 minutes before serving; if you're refrigerating the cake longer, allow some time for the frosting to come to room temperature before serving. With a sharp knife, cut the cake into thick wedges. Celebrate!

Repertoire Chocolate Cake

Makes one 8-inch layer cake

1 cup unsalted butter,
plus more for greasing the pans

12 tablespoons (2½ ounces)
Dutch process cocoa powder

2 teaspoons instant
espresso powder

⅔ cup boiling water

⅔ cup milk

2 cups cake flour

1 teaspoon baking soda

½ teaspoon baking powder

½ teaspoon kosher salt

2 cups sugar

3 eggs, at room temperature

1 teaspoon vanilla extract

FOR THE FROSTING:

1 cup heavy cream

8 ounces good-quality milk
chocolate, chopped

8 ounces semisweet chocolate
(64 percent), chopped

1 cup unsalted butter, at room
temperature, cubed

Pinch of kosher salt

Chocolate sprinkles (optional)

THERE AREN'T a whole lot of things that I am dogmatic about, but layer cakes are one of them (as evidenced by these back-to-back cake recipes). Baking a layer cake is an act of love, and, more than almost any other recipe in this book, this chocolate cake is something I think everyone should have in his or her repertoire.

It's an ideal birthday cake and I believe (again with the cake dogma) that birthday cakes should always be made at home. Since I've begun doing the birthday-party circuit with my own children, I've seen a lot of beautiful cakes—professional bakery cakes piped with buttercream rosettes, sheet cakes topped with mises-en-scène that would put some off-Broadway sets to shame. It's not that those cakes don't taste good; I often eat more than my fair share. But I have a deep fondness for leaning homemade layer cakes, for cupcakes smeared hastily with frosting and showered with colored sprinkles. To me, the lifelong recipient of a homemade birthday cake every year (thanks, Mom), those funky cakes are love made visible.

I have made dozens and dozens of chocolate cakes in my life, but this recipe is the only one I'll use from now on. It has a delicate crumb and is almost jet black because of the generous amount of cocoa powder. The silky chocolate frosting seems like it will be impossibly rich but it's just right, and it spreads so easily that even if this is the first cake you've ever frosted, it's going to look beautiful.

The cake can also be baked as cupcakes; reduce the baking time to 18 minutes. It will make 18, enough for whatever school function or potluck you've promised to supply dessert for. Any extra frosting can be frozen.

> Place a rack in the center of the oven and preheat the oven to 350°F. Butter two 8-inch round cake pans and line the bottom of each pan with parchment paper. Butter the parchment and dust the

pan with cocoa powder; tap out the excess.

> In a medium bowl, whisk together the cocoa, espresso powder, and boiling water. Whisk in the milk and let cool.

> Sift together the cake flour, baking soda, baking powder, and salt. Set aside.

> In an electric mixer fitted with the paddle attachment, beat the 1 cup butter and sugar until light and fluffy, about 5 minutes. Beat in the eggs one at a time, then beat in the vanilla. With the mixer on low speed, gradually pour in the cooled cocoa mixture and mix until fully incorporated. Gradually add the sifted dry ingredients to the chocolate mixture, mixing until just combined.

> Pour the batter into the prepared pans. Bake for 15 minutes, rotate the pans, and bake for an additional 15 to 20 minutes, until a toothpick inserted into the center of the cake comes out clean. Remove the layers from the oven, and allow them to cool in pans for 15 minutes on a cooling rack.

Carefully run a small offset spatula around the edges of the layers to loosen them from the pans. Remove them from the pans, and invert onto a wire rack. Let cool completely, about 1 hour. The cake can be made a day ahead; once cool, wrap each layer tightly in plastic wrap and refrigerate. The cooled layers can also be tightly wrapped and frozen for up to a month.

> **WHILE THE LAYERS COOL, MAKE THE FROSTING:** Heat the cream in a small saucepan until bubbles form at the edges of the pan. Put the chocolate in a large heatproof bowl and pour the cream over; let stand 5 minutes, then whisk until smooth. Whisk in the cubed butter until the mixture is smooth and silky. Let cool at room temperature; the frosting will thicken but remain spreadable. The frosting can be made up to a week ahead and refrigerated; let come to room temperature before using.

> If the tops of the cake layers have mounded unevenly, level them by removing the top crust with a long serrated knife. With a serrated knife, cut each cake layer in half horizontally to create two thin layers.

> Place one cake layer on a cake stand or large plate and top with about $1/2$ cup of the frosting, spreading in an even layer all the way to the edges. Top with a second cake layer and another $1/2$ cup frosting. Repeat with the next 2 layers. With an offset spatula, spread the remaining frosting in a thick layer over the top and sides of the cake, using the tip of the spatula to create decorative curls and swirls. Decorate the top and sides of the frosted cake with sprinkles, if using, pressing lightly to adhere. Refrigerate the cake at least 15 minutes before serving; if you're refrigerating the cake longer, allow some time for the frosting to come to room temperature before serving. With a sharp knife, cut the cake into thick wedges.

S'Mores Tart

Makes one 9-inch tart

12 graham cracker sheets

¾ cup sugar

6 tablespoons unsalted butter, melted

Pinch of kosher salt

8 ounces good-quality milk chocolate, finely chopped

4 ounces good-quality semisweet chocolate (64 percent), finely chopped

1½ cups heavy cream

2 teaspoons vanilla extract

¼ cup egg whites (from 2 large eggs)

¼ cup light corn syrup

THE COMBINATION of graham crackers, chocolate, and toasted marshmallow is unbeatable. Like the campfire snack that inspired it, this tart is beloved by children and, if you're the type of person who likes to bake with your kids (which means you are a better, more patient person than I), then this is a recipe you might tackle together—those sweaty little fingers can press the crumbs into the tart pan to form the crust and stir together warm cream and chocolate until smooth. And children are suitably impressed by the sight of egg whites and sugar become marshmallow right before their eyes, but be warned: my boys always manage to get some in their hair.

> Preheat the oven to 375°F. Pulse the graham crackers in a food processor until fine; you should have 1½ cups graham cracker crumbs. Transfer to a bowl, add ¼ cup of the sugar, melted butter, and salt and mix until well combined. Press evenly into a 9-inch removable-bottom tart pan. Transfer to the oven and bake until golden, 10 minutes. Remove from the oven and let cool.

> Put the chocolate in a heatproof bowl. Heat the cream in a small saucepan over medium heat without stirring until bubbles form at the edges of the pan. Pour the hot cream over the chocolate and let stand 1 minute, then stir until smooth. Stir in 1 teaspoon of the vanilla. Pour into the prepared crust and refrigerate until set, 2 hours.

> MAKE THE MARSHMALLOW TOPPING: Combine the egg whites, remaining ½ cup sugar, corn syrup, and remaining 1 teaspoon vanilla in a heatproof bowl and place over a saucepan of simmering water. Whisk the egg-white mixture until the sugar dissolves, 2 to 3 minutes, then transfer to an electric mixer fitted with the whisk attachment and beat until it has increased dramatically in volume and is light and fluffy, about 5 minutes. (You can also do this with a hand mixer.) Remove the tart from the refrigerator and spread the marshmallow over the chocolate, leaving the crust exposed. The tart can be broiled and served right away, or you can return it to the refrigerator and chill for up to 3 hours.

> Just before serving, preheat the broiler. Put the tart under the broiler a few inches from the heating element and broil with the oven door slightly ajar until the marshmallow is toasty brown, watching carefully so it doesn't burn (alternatively, you can use a kitchen torch to brown the marshmallow). Carefully remove the tart from the pan and transfer to a serving platter. Cut into thin wedges with a hot knife.

THE THREE GREATEST COOKIES

Chocolate Chip Cookies

Makes 24 cookies

4¼ cups all-purpose flour

1¼ teaspoons kosher salt

1¼ teaspoons baking soda

1¼ teaspoons baking powder

1¼ cups unsalted butter, at room temperature

1¼ cups dark brown sugar

1 cup plus 2 tablespoons granulated sugar

2 large eggs

1½ teaspoons vanilla extract

1 pound semisweet chocolate chips

SPENT A LONG TIME deciding whether or not to include my recipe for these cookies in this book. On the one hand, they are a cornerstone of my repertoire. We always have a bag of dough balls in the freezer, ready to bake, and I am always in the mood for a chocolate chip cookie. On the other hand, the world is saturated with chocolate chip cookie recipes—do you really need another?

But let me tell you, folks: I buy chocolate chip cookies almost every time I see them, at bakeries and coffee shops around the country. And the vast majority of them are not even close to as good as the ones I make at home. Not even close! So maybe there is something about this recipe after all. Credit really goes to my wife, who tweaked this formula over the years until it was perfect, yielding cookies with crispy edges and soft, chewy middles, shot through with plenty of good chocolate.

> In a large bowl, whisk together the flour, salt, baking soda, and baking powder.

> In the bowl of an electric mixer fitted with the paddle attachment, combine the butter, brown sugar, and granulated sugar and beat on high speed until light and fluffy, about 3 minutes. Stop the mixer and scrape down the sides of the bowl with a rubber spatula. With the mixer on medium speed, add the eggs one at a time, followed by the vanilla.

> Reduce the mixer speed to low and gradually add the dry ingredients, mixing until combined. Remove the bowl from the mixer and fold in the chocolate chips.

> Preheat the oven to 375°F. Line two rimmed baking sheets with silicone baking mats or parchment paper. Using an ice cream scoop or a tablespoon, scoop the dough and roll into balls slightly larger than a golf ball (about 2 ounces each). Transfer the balls to the prepared baking sheets, spacing them about 2 inches apart. Transfer the pans to the oven and bake until the cookies are golden brown on the edges but still

RECIPE CONTINUES ↘

soft at the center, around 10 to 12 minutes. About a minute before the cookies are done, I do something weird: I lift each pan about an inch off the oven rack and drop it down with a thud. The cookies deflate, and I'm convinced this is what gives them their excellent chewy texture. It could be my imagination, but try it and see what you think.

> Remove from the oven and let cool for a minute on the baking sheets, then use a spatula to transfer the cookies to a wire rack and let cool. Repeat with the remaining dough, or transfer the remaining dough balls to a rimmed pan and freeze; when frozen solid, transfer to a plastic freezer storage bag. The cookies will keep for up to a month in the freezer.

I like to let them thaw on the baking sheet for about 10 minutes before baking; add 1 to 2 minutes to the total baking time.

Chewy Molasses Cookies

Makes 18 cookies

12 tablespoons unsalted butter, at room temperature

1 cup packed dark brown sugar

¼ cup unsulfured molasses (not blackstrap)

1 large egg

2¼ cups all-purpose flour

2 teaspoons baking soda

1½ teaspoons ground cinnamon

1½ teaspoons ground ginger

½ teaspoon kosher salt

Sanding sugar or granulated sugar, for rolling

THE RECIPE for these spicy, soft cookies comes from my mother-in-law. They are just right dunked in coffee, they are just right for ice cream sandwiching…they are just right. If you want, skip the step of rolling the cookies in sugar and instead drizzle them with a glaze (half a cup of confectioners' sugar to two teaspoons milk, whisked until smooth) after they've baked and cooled. *(Pictured on page 200.)*

⎯⎯

> Preheat the oven to 375°F and line two rimmed baking sheets with silicone baking mats or parchment paper. In the bowl of an electric mixer fitted with the paddle attachment, combine the butter and brown sugar. Beat on medium-high speed until creamy, 3 to 4 minutes. Reduce the speed to low and mix in the molasses and egg until combined.

> In a medium bowl, whisk together the flour, baking soda, cinnamon, ginger, and salt. With the mixer on low, gradually add the dry ingredients until combined.

> Pour some sanding or granulated sugar on a plate. With your hands, roll the dough into balls slightly larger than a golf ball (about 2 ounces; if the dough is sticking to your hands, wet them), then roll each ball in sugar to coat. Transfer to the prepared baking sheets and use the bottom of a juice glass to gently flatten each cookie. Bake, rotating the pans midway through the baking time, until flattened and cracked on top, about 10 minutes. Transfer to a wire cooling rack and let cool on the pan for a few minutes, then use a spatula to transfer the cookies to the rack and let cool completely.

Cocoa-Oat Cookies

Makes about 16 cookies

1½ cups all-purpose flour

½ cup white rice flour

½ cup Dutch process cocoa powder

1 teaspoon baking powder

1 teaspoon baking soda

1 teaspoon kosher salt

8 tablespoons unsalted butter, at room temperature

1 cup light brown sugar

½ cup white sugar

2 eggs

1 teaspoon vanilla extract

1⅓ cups rolled oats

1 cup finely shredded unsweetened coconut

3 ounces good-quality bittersweet chocolate (74 percent), finely chopped

IT STARTED INNOCENTLY ENOUGH. Tired of disappointing oatmeal-raisin cookies, I set out to perfect a recipe that addressed my own oatmeal-raisin-related peculiarities. But, well, what can I say—I got distracted. I started to think about chocolate crinkle cookies, dark and rich with cocoa. I thought about my love of chocolate-dipped coconut macaroons, and Dorie Greenspan's dark-chocolate-studded World Peace Cookies. (If you don't know, Google it. You're welcome.)

Before I knew it, I no longer had anything resembling an oatmeal-raisin cookie, but I had these rich, fudgy numbers, shot through with coconut. The small amount of rice flour in this dough might seem like a fiddly detail, but it contributes enormously to the soft, chewy texture of the cookie. It's vital that you don't overbake these cookies; if you do, they'll go from soft and chewy to dry and crumbly. Pull them out when they still look a bit underbaked.

> Preheat the oven to 350°F and line two rimmed baking sheets with parchment paper or silicone baking mats. In a medium bowl, whisk together the all-purpose and rice flours, cocoa powder, baking powder, baking soda, and salt.

> In the bowl of an electric mixer fitted with a paddle attachment beat the butter, brown sugar, and white sugar on medium-high speed until light and fluffy, about 5 minutes. Reduce the speed to low and add the eggs one at a time, beating after each addition, then add the vanilla and mix to combine. Gradually add the dry ingredients and mix until combined, then add the oats, coconut, and chocolate and mix until incorporated.

> Roll the dough into balls that are slightly larger than golf balls (about 2 ounces each). Arrange on the baking sheets, spacing the balls about 2 inches apart. Bake for 7 minutes, then use a spatula to gently flatten each cookie and bake for about 6 minutes more, until they are cracked on top and look just set but not dry. Do not overbake. Let cool on the pans for 1 minute, then use a spatula to transfer to a wire rack and let cool completely.

Ultimate Chocolate Ice Cream *with* Cinnamon Bread Crumbs

Makes 1 quart ice cream

4 ounces semisweet chocolate (64 percent), chopped

1¾ cups heavy cream

¼ cup Dutch process cocoa

1 cup 1 percent or 2 percent milk

¾ cup sugar

5 egg yolks

1 teaspoon vanilla extract

THIS IS INTENSE chocolate ice cream that owes its flavor to a double hit of cocoa and chocolate. It's perfect on its own, but you could also mix in anything from finely chopped candied orange peel to marshmallows and toasted walnuts to crushed candy canes. But I like it with a topping for which I have my friend Chad Robertson to thank.

Chad, a master baker, taught me to put crunchy, salty, oil-slicked bread crumbs inside my omelets, one of those genius moves that change everything, and also introduced me to sweet bread crumbs fried in butter and cinnamon until toasty. Here I treat them like sprinkles, spooning them liberally over a bowl of ice cream or rolling the top of my cone in them to coat.

There are many brands of great store-bought ice cream. But when you realize how simple it is to make a really tremendous version at home using a countertop ice cream maker, there's no going back.

> Put the chocolate in a medium bowl. In a medium saucepan over medium heat, whisk together the heavy cream and cocoa. Cook, whisking, until the cream is hot but not boiling, then pour over the chopped chocolate. Let stand for 1 minute, then whisk until smooth. Set aside.

> Pour the milk into a medium saucepan (you can use the same one that you used for the cream and chocolate) and add 6 tablespoons of the sugar. Cook over medium heat, stirring, until the milk is hot. In a medium bowl, whisk together the egg yolks and the remaining 6 tablespoons of sugar until well combined. Whisking constantly, pour in half of the hot milk mixture and continue whisking until mixed. Pour the egg-yolk mixture into the saucepan with the remaining milk and cook over medium heat, stirring constantly with a rubber spatula or wooden spoon, until the custard thickens enough to coat the back of a spoon, about 5 minutes.

> Pour through a fine-mesh sieve into the bowl containing the chocolate mixture and stir to combine. Set the bowl in an ice bath and let stand, stirring occasionally, until cool. Wrap the bowl tightly with plastic wrap and refrigerate overnight.

Stir in the vanilla extract and churn in an ice cream maker according to the manufacturer's instructions. Transfer to a freezer-safe storage vessel (I find quart-size yogurt containers to be perfect) and freeze until firm.

Cinnamon Bread Crumbs

Y ou can make these bread crumbs with either fresh or slightly stale bread (it's a good way to use up the stump of a loaf). Take some care in the toasting, otherwise you'll end up with a topping that's more chewy than crunchy.

2 tablespoons unsalted butter

1 cup fresh bread crumbs made from challah, brioche, white sandwich bread, or other soft, sweet bread

½ teaspoon sugar

½ teaspoon ground cinnamon

Pinch of salt

———

> Melt the butter in a small frying pan over medium-low heat, then stir in the bread crumbs. Sprinkle with the sugar, cinnamon, and salt and cook, stirring, until the bread crumbs are very dry and crunchy.

> Remove from the heat and let cool, then transfer to a bowl. (If you want finer crumbs—to roll an ice cream cone in, for example—transfer the cooled crumbs to a plastic zip-top storage bag and crush with a rolling pin.) The bread crumbs are best the same day they are made.

Creamsicle Affogato

Serves 1

2 ounces freshly squeezed orange juice

1 large scoop vanilla ice cream

Candied orange peel, for garnish (optional)

THIS IS LESS OF A RECIPE and more of a suggestion for a smart thing you can do with ice cream. Inspired by the original Italian affogato, hot espresso poured over vanilla ice cream, this California version uses hot orange juice instead. If you grew up going to Orange Julius, or if you once smoked pot and ate frozen orange-juice concentrate straight from the tube in your friend's kitchen, you'll enjoy this one-two combo.

———

> Pour the juice into a small saucepan and heat over low heat. Scoop the ice cream into a glass or small bowl. When the juice is hot, immediately pour it over the ice cream. Garnish with candied orange peel, if using. Eat immediately.

Vanilla Bread Pudding *with* Cognac Prunes *and* Dark Chocolate

Serves 8 to 10

½ cup finely chopped dried pitted prunes

½ cup cognac or other brandy

3 cups heavy cream

1 vanilla bean

5 packed cups cubed soft white bread, such as pain de mie, challah, brioche, or white sandwich bread, cut into 1-inch cubes

4 large eggs

¾ cup sugar

½ teaspoon kosher salt

1 teaspoon vanilla extract

2 ounces semisweet (64 percent) chocolate, coarsely chopped

WHEN I WAS LIVING IN Cambridge, Massachusetts, there was a restaurant halfway between my house and Formaggio Kitchen, where I worked, that I'd walk by twice a day. It was a neighborhood bistro, nothing special, but I have distinct memories of walking home on cold winter nights and catching a whiff of steak on the grill that heralded the end of my work day. The restaurant also made a superlative bread pudding. I tried to get the recipe a few times, but they wouldn't share it, and one day, the restaurant closed.

I did my best to replicate the recipe here, though I took some liberties and added chunks of chocolate, which melt into puddles when the pudding is baked, and cognac-soaked prunes, which punctuate the gentle custard with their boozy sweetness.

———

> Put the prunes in a bowl and pour the cognac over. Let soak at least 2 hours and up to 3 weeks.

> Pour the heavy cream into a medium heavy-bottomed saucepan. Split the vanilla bean lengthwise and use the tip of a knife to scrape out the seeds. Add the vanilla seeds and pod to the cream and heat over medium heat until small bubbles begin to form at the edges of the pan (do not let it boil). Remove from heat, cover, and let stand 30 minutes. Remove the vanilla-bean pod and discard (alternatively, you can rinse the pod, dry it, and combine it with sugar to make vanilla-scented sugar).

> Spread the cubed bread in a 9-inch-by-13-inch glass or metal baking dish in an even layer. In an electric mixer, beat the eggs, sugar, and salt until light, fluffy, and voluminous, about 5 minutes. Pour in the heavy cream and vanilla extract and mix to combine. Pour the custard through a fine-mesh sieve over the cubed bread. Gently nudge the bread down into the custard.

> Drain the prunes, reserving the liquid (it makes a killer cocktail). Sprinkle the prunes and chopped chocolate over the surface of the custard and use your fingertips to press the chocolate and prunes down into the custard. Refrigerate for 30 minutes.

> Preheat the oven to 350°F and bring a kettle of water to a boil. Set the bread-pudding dish into a larger roasting pan and add enough hot water to the roasting pan so it comes halfway up the side of the dish. Transfer to the oven and bake until the custard is just set, about 45 minutes. Remove from the oven and let cool. Once cool, the bread pudding can be covered and refrigerated overnight (if you've made it ahead, set it in a low oven for 15 minutes until warmed through, then broil the top as described below).

> Just before serving, preheat the broiler. Put the bread pudding under the broiler, about 3 inches from the heating element, and broil until the top of the bread pudding is nicely browned. Do not leave the pudding unattended or the top may burn. Remove from the oven and let cool for 5 minutes, then cut the bread pudding into squares and serve warm.

Rice Pudding

with Citrus *and* Pistachios

Serves 6

2½ cups whole milk

2 cups half-and-half

½ cup sugar

Pinch of kosher salt

One 2-inch stick cinnamon

2 cardamom pods, crushed

½ vanilla bean, split lengthwise, seeds scraped

⅓ cup long-grain white rice (I like jasmine)

1 egg yolk

½ teaspoon orange zest

3 oranges

1 teaspoon rose water (optional)

3 tablespoons toasted salted pistachios, coarsely chopped

TRUE STORY: I once wrote a letter to Kozy Shack complaining that its rice pudding did not contain enough rice. I take pudding seriously. And though this is sort of an old-fashioned dessert, it's about as comforting as they come.

I take a hard line against raisins in rice pudding, and I lace mine judiciously with cinnamon (whole sticks, not ground) and cardamom. The citrus salad and pistachios are just one option—you can serve the pudding unadorned or with another toasted nut or fruit. It'd be great topped with the strawberry compote on page 180.

> In a large heavy-bottomed saucepan, combine 2 cups of the milk, the half-and-half, sugar, salt, cinnamon stick, cardamom pods, and vanilla bean and seeds. Stir in the rice. Bring to a boil over medium-high heat, then reduce to a simmer. Cover and simmer for 15 minutes. Uncover and continue cooking, stirring frequently, until the rice is tender and the mixture is beginning to thicken, 15 minutes more.

> In a small bowl, whisk together the remaining ½ cup milk, the egg yolk, and the orange zest. Add a spoonful of the hot rice mixture and stir vigorously, then pour into the pot with the remaining rice pudding. Cook, stirring constantly, until the mixture coats the back of a spoon, about 5 minutes more. Remove and discard the cinnamon stick, cardamom pods, and vanilla bean. Transfer to a bowl and press a sheet of plastic wrap directly onto the surface of the pudding. Refrigerate until cold.

> Cut the ends off each orange and, with a sharp knife, following the contour of the fruit, cut the peel and pith off each orange. Working over a bowl, hold the orange in your nondominant hand and use a sharp knife to cut each segment of fruit free from the membrane, letting it drop into the bowl beneath. Add the rose water to the bowl with the orange segments and mix very gently to combine. Refrigerate until ready to serve.

> To serve, spoon some of the pudding into a bowl. Top with some of the orange supremes and their juice and some of the pistachios. Serve.

Glazed Gingerbread Cake

Makes one 9-inch cake

2 cups all-purpose flour

2½ teaspoons ground ginger

1½ teaspoons ground nutmeg

1 teaspoon baking soda

¾ teaspoon ground cloves

1 teaspoon baking powder

½ teaspoon ground cinnamon

½ teaspoon kosher salt

¼ teaspoon ground black pepper

4 tablespoons unsalted butter, at room temperature

1 cup packed plus 2 tablespoons packed light brown sugar

2 large eggs

½ cup crème fraîche or sour cream

1 ounce grated fresh ginger (peeled before grating)

7 tablespoons unsulfured molasses (not blackstrap) dissolved in ½ cup hot water

2 tablespoons finely chopped candied ginger

FOR THE GLAZE:

¾ cup confectioners' sugar

1 tablespoon plus 1 teaspoon milk

½ teaspoon vanilla extract

I AM REALLY PARTICULAR about gingerbread, even though it's a humble dessert. I believe that good gingerbread should be moist enough that it sticks to your fingers a bit if you're eating it with your hands and that it should have enough ginger and black pepper to make it a little spicy. So committed was I to creating the ultimate gingerbread that I tested almost a dozen variations on this recipe; for a while, I was bringing gingerbread everywhere I went, giving wedges to the UPS man, the teachers at my kids' school, and all our neighbors.

This gingerbread falls into the category of sweets that I call snack cakes, meaning it's appropriate at any time of day (especially breakfast). Most gingerbread recipes are made with oil, but mine is made with butter and crème fraîche, which give the finished cake an especially delicate, tender crumb and great flavor. It also tastes richly of ginger, which appears in the recipe in three forms: fresh, powdered, and candied.

› Preheat the oven to 350°F. Grease and flour a 9-inch round pan and line the bottom with parchment paper. Grease the parchment. Set aside. In a medium bowl, sift together the flour, ginger, nutmeg, baking soda, ground cloves, baking powder, cinnamon, salt, and black pepper.

› In an electric mixer fitted with the paddle attachment, beat the butter on medium-high speed until creamy, then add the brown sugar and beat until blended. Reduce the speed to medium and add the eggs one at a time, beating until smooth, then beat in the crème fraîche and grated fresh ginger. Reduce the mixer speed to low and add the dry ingredients in 3 batches, alternating with the molasses mixture, beginning and ending with the dry ingredients. Mix in the candied ginger.

› Transfer the batter to the prepared pan. Bake until a tester inserted in the center of the cake comes out clean, about 45 to 50 minutes. Transfer to a wire rack and let cool 15 minutes, then turn out of the pan and let cool completely.

RECIPE CONTINUES ↘

> **MAKE THE GLAZE:** In a medium bowl, whisk together the confectioners' sugar, milk, and vanilla until smooth. When the cake is completely cool, pour the glaze over it, letting some run down the sides. Cut into thick wedges and serve plain or with whipped cream.

Maple-Blueberry Cornmeal Cake

Makes one 9-inch cake

1 cup dark amber maple syrup

13 tablespoons unsalted butter, at room temperature

2 cups blueberries

1½ cups all-purpose flour

½ cup coarse cornmeal

1½ teaspoons baking powder

1 teaspoon kosher salt

½ teaspoon baking soda

3 eggs

¾ cup buttermilk

1 teaspoon vanilla extract

1 cup plus 2 tablespoons sugar

Crème fraîche or vanilla ice cream, for serving

WHILE MY FATHER might not be a great cook, he loves good food, and he introduced me to some of the finer tastes in life, including Ritz crackers spread with both unsalted butter *and* Jif peanut butter (a technique we call "double buttered" in our family). Dad was also responsible for one of my favorite childhood breakfasts: crumbled leftover corn bread, toasted in the oven, then generously dotted with salted butter and doused in real maple syrup. This cake, which tastes a lot like that breakfast, is for my dad.

> Preheat the oven to 350°F. Put the maple syrup in a small saucepan over medium heat. Bring to a boil and cook until the syrup has reduced by half. Remove from the heat and stir in 1 tablespoon of the butter (the mixture may crystallize, but this is okay), then pour into a 9-inch-by-3-inch round cake pan and tilt the pan so that the syrup coats the bottom evenly. Arrange the berries in a single layer on top.

> In a medium bowl, whisk together the flour, cornmeal, baking powder, salt, and baking soda. In a separate bowl, whisk together the eggs, buttermilk, and vanilla.

> In an electric mixer fitted with the paddle attachment (or a large bowl with a handheld mixer), beat the remaining 12 tablespoons of butter and the sugar on high speed until fluffy. Reduce the mixer speed to low and alternate additions of dry and wet ingredients. Mix until the batter is smooth, scraping down the bowl as needed.

> Transfer the batter to the pan and smooth the top. Bake until the cake is golden brown and pulling from the edges of the pan and a cake tester inserted in the center comes out clean, 1 hour. Cool for 10 minutes on a wire rack, then run a thin knife or offset spatula around the edges of the pan and turn the cake out onto the rack. Let cool completely, then transfer to a platter. Cut into wedges and serve with a spoonful of crème fraîche or ice cream. The cake is also very good for breakfast.

Sweet *and* Tart Lemon Bars

Makes 20 small bars

FOR THE CRUST:

1 cup unsalted butter, at room temperature

½ cup granulated sugar

1¾ cups all-purpose flour

½ teaspoon kosher salt

FOR THE FILLING:

5 whole eggs

1 egg yolk

1⅔ cups sugar

3 tablespoons all-purpose flour

Pinch of kosher salt

1 cup lemon juice (from 5 to 6 large lemons)

1 tablespoon lemon zest (from 2 lemons)

2 tablespoons heavy cream

Confectioners' sugar, for dusting

A LARGE PART of developing one's repertoire lies in tweaking recipes to suit one's own taste. I love lemon bars but could never understand why the majority of those I purchased from bakeries were sickly sweet or, worse, had an aroma that reminded me of a wet dog. Well, I guess if you want something done right, you have to do it yourself, so I set out to make my ultimate lemon bar, one with a pronounced tartness and a tender, shortbread-like crust. This recipe is the result of my efforts. A friend of mine, pastry chef Elisabeth Prueitt, likes her lemon bars ice cold from the fridge. This is a pro move, so I'm seconding her suggestion here. Don't worry if the surface of your baked lemon bars is pocked with air bubbles; this is totally normal and will be covered by a final dusting of confectioners' sugar.

――――

> Preheat the oven to 350°F. Line a 9-inch-by-13-inch baking pan with parchment paper, leaving some overhang on both of the short ends of the pan (this will make it easier to remove the bars from the pan). In the bowl of a mixer fitted with the paddle attachment (or in a large bowl with a handheld mixer), cream the butter and sugar on high speed until light and fluffy, about 2 minutes. Reduce the mixer speed to low and add the flour and salt. Mix until the dough comes together into a ball. With your fingers, press the dough into the prepared pan in an even layer. Transfer to the oven and bake until golden brown, about 20 to 25 minutes. Transfer to a wire rack and reduce the oven temperature to 325°F.

> WHILE THE CRUST BAKES, MAKE THE FILLING: In a large bowl, whisk together the eggs, egg yolk, sugar, flour, and salt until smooth. Whisk in the lemon juice and zest and the heavy cream. Pour over the warm crust, then return to the oven and bake just until the lemon mixture is set, about 20 minutes. Remove from the oven and let cool completely on a wire rack (if you want to try them chilled, pop the pan into the fridge once it's cooled to room temperature). Just before serving, dust with a generous snowdrift of confectioners' sugar and cut into bars.

Perfect Tarte Tatin

Makes one 10-inch tart

FOR THE DOUGH:

1¼ cups all-purpose flour

2 teaspoons sugar

½ teaspoon kosher salt

9 tablespoons cold unsalted butter, cubed

¼ cup ice-cold water

....

5 pounds sweet-tart firm apples (about 12), such as Pink Lady or Braeburn (avoid Granny Smiths)

8 tablespoons unsalted butter

1½ cups granulated sugar

Homemade Crème Fraîche, for serving

THIS APPLE TART is one of my very favorite things to bake (and eat). I learned the recipe for this French classic, fittingly, when I was living in France. I'd tasted versions of it before, but it wasn't until I was taught to make it by Anne Willan that I really understood how amazing it could be. The key to this recipe is to cook the caramel until it's a deep brown, so dark that you think you might be on the verge of totally fucking it up.

At that moment, you quickly lower the heat and add the apples to the pan. The most miraculous thing happens—the juice from the apples stops the caramel from burning and becoming acrid, and, over the next thirty minutes, the apples continue to release their juices while sucking up the caramel. By the time you pull the pan from the stove and add the pastry, the apple halves are jewel-like, mahogany, and the apple juice–fortified caramel is sticky and complex. After making this tart more times than I can count, I've noticed that the variety of apple you use makes a difference. Most firm-tart varieties will work, but Granny Smiths seem to get especially mushy, so I avoid those.

The dessert is a showstopper and, I think, handily kicks apple pie to the curb. I like to serve wedges of it topped with tangy crème fraîche. The caramel can make the pastry soggy if it sits for a while, so I recommend eating this on the same day it's made.

> MAKE THE DOUGH: Combine the flour, sugar, and salt in the bowl of a food processor and pulse to combine. Add the butter and pulse until the butter pieces are about half the size of a pea. Slowly add ice water, 1 tablespoon at a time, and pulse until the dough just comes together.

> Turn the dough out onto a lightly floured surface and gather into a ball. Flatten into a disk, then wrap tightly with plastic wrap and refrigerate for at least 1 hour and up to 2 days, or freeze for up to 2 months. Thaw overnight in the refrigerator before using.

> Peel the apples. With a melon baller, scoop out the stem and blossom ends. Halve the apple and use the

RECIPE CONTINUES ↘

melon baller to scoop out the cores. Melt the butter in a 10-inch cast-iron or other high-sided ovenproof frying pan over medium heat and add the sugar. Cook without stirring until the mixture begins to brown at its edges, then stir gently and continue cooking until the caramel is a deep golden brown, about 6 minutes more. This takes some courage; you want the caramel to be very dark but not scorched. As it approaches the correct color, reduce the heat to low and put a spoon along the edge of the pan with the bowl of the spoon facing down. Arrange the apple halves in concentric circles, leaning the first apple half against the spoon so it doesn't topple over. Pack the apples as tightly as possible, cutting some into wedges to fill in the gaps, as they will shrink during cooking.

> Increase the heat to medium and cook until the apples begin to exude their juices (this will be fairly obvious, as the level of caramel in the pan will rise to almost halfway up each piece of apple), about 6 minutes, then raise the heat to medium high

and cook until the undersides of the apples are deeply caramelized and tender but not mushy and the juices are sticky and thickened, about 10 to 12 minutes more. Using two spoons, turn the apple halves one at a time so the upper sides are now down in the caramel. Continue cooking until this second side is caramelized and almost all the juice has evaporated and what remains in the pan is syrupy, about 10 minutes longer. The apples should be tender but not mushy. Remove the pan from the heat and let cool slightly. Preheat the oven to 400°F.

> On a lightly floured work surface with a lightly floured rolling pin, roll the chilled dough into a 12-inch circle and trim the edges. Set the pastry on top of the apples, tucking the pastry edges down into the pan, then cut a few steam vents in the pastry. Bake for 20 to 25 minutes, until the pastry is golden brown. Remove from the oven and let cool for 10 minutes, then invert a large, rimmed plate on top of the tart and flip the tart onto the plate. Let cool until warm (or cool completely and

rewarm in a low oven before serving), then cut into wedges and serve with big spoonfuls of crème fraîche.

Homemade Crème Fraîche

Though it's no longer terribly difficult to find crème fraîche at the grocery store (I have even seen it at Costco), making it at home is easy and inexpensive. Tangy and thick, it's an excellent companion to the tarte tatin (and many other things, including the potato pancakes on page 72).

Makes about 1 cup

1 cup heavy cream

1 tablespoon cultured buttermilk or plain yogurt

———

> Combine the cream and buttermilk or yogurt in a clean glass jar. Cover and let stand at room temperature about 10 to 12 hours, until thickened. Refrigerate for up to 2 weeks.

Acknowledgments

I hit the jackpot in the family lottery. I'm grateful to my parents, who probably saw this book coming long before I did, and to my brother and sister, who are always there when I need them.

I knew the first time that I spoke with him, while standing in a Target parking lot in Emeryville, California, that Mike Szczerban would be both a great editor and a great friend. He just gets it. Thanks, Mike.

I owe a huge debt of gratitude to Jenny Wapner, as brilliant a cheerleader and as loving a friend as you could find and someone who has believed in *Repertoire* since the earliest days. I'm also thankful to my agent, Kim Witherspoon, who is the very definition of a smooth operator.

Christian Reynoso patiently cooked *Repertoire* recipes alongside me for months and months, during which time he became a trusted sounding board and a great pal. Christian, you're the coolest. Thanks to Paolo Lucchesi for supporting my Repertoire column at the *San Francisco Chronicle*.

I had many, many testers who believed in this book enough to make these recipes in their home kitchens. Thanks to Marni Berger, Vijay Ram, Bettyann Chun, Tessa Tyler, Jennifer Guest, Anne Jung, Jennifer Baron, Mandy Morris, Leigh Hermansen, Alicia Prodromou, Jessie Li, Katie Colendich, Victoria Wollard, Jennifer Kinion, Hannah Furgerson, Jennifer Durning, Caleb Zigas, Anna Kohl, Brennan Dates, John and Will Gransky, Lena Zuckerwise, Sasha Bernstein, Anne Dailey, and Thea Anderson. The book is better for your help (see, we really tested these recipes!).

Ed Anderson has a mellow disposition, a great eye, and a well-developed sense of sarcasm, all qualities that make him a great photographer (and friend). Thanks for making this book so beautiful, Ed. Next Woodstock Negroni is on me. And thanks to Sam Mogannam, Anne Walker, Lena Corwin, and Josh Dreier, who lent me their homes for photo shoots.

Toni Tajima, you complete my cookbook dream team. Thank you for contributing your considerable talent to the design of this book.

Ellis and Sidney, you are my most honest critics. Long after I'm gone, I hope you'll cook the recipes in this book for your own kids.

And to my wife, Sarah: None of this would be possible without you. Thank you. I love you.

Index

Page numbers in *italics* refer to photographs.

About the Author

Jessica Battilana writes the Repertoire column for the *San Francisco Chronicle* and is the author of *Corn,* from Short Stack Editions. She is also the coauthor of several other cookbooks, and her work has appeared in *Martha Stewart Living,* the *New York Times,* the *Wall Street Journal, Gastronomica, Saveur, Sunset,* and multiple editions of *Best Food Writing.* A Vermont native, she lives in San Francisco with her wife and children.

11/93